how
TO BE A BETTER
foodie

how
TO BE A BETTER
foodie

a BULGING
little book
FOR THE
truly
epicurious

SUDI PIGOTT

Illustrations by Paul Bommer

Quadrille

Contents

Introduction

Frankly, I'm proud to be a fully committed Foodie and absolutely not afraid of the F-word.

Whilst friends and family have (mostly) kept their thoughts about my increasingly bulging waistline to themselves, they've become palpably more intrigued by my passionate immersion in shopping, eating, reading, holidaying and conversing obsessively about food – and rather more keen to have what I'm having.

The prophetic might call this a gastro-epiphany and it seems it's not a passing Foodie phase, but a widely felt need for a little something tasty to explain just how to become a Better Foodie.

Personally, I can trace my unalloyed pleasure in good eating back to my childhood. I first developed foodietude through licking the maple and walnut sponge cake bowl. Luckily my mother believed, and still believes, there's no point in teatime without proper homemade cake. Yet, I've only realised recently that this explains my 'catillating' inclination – an affliction fulsome

Foodies are prone to – that is my unspeakably rude, yet delicious habit of licking plates with my little finger!

There's no perfect stage in life to become a Better Foodie. It can get you young: aged eight, I was already preparing Foodie feasts for my fortunate posse of soft toys – mostly mini bridge rolls with smoked salmon, malt loaf and squidgy peppermint creams. My eleven-year-old son is busy converting his friends to single-estate 'proper' chocolate and proud of his nigri sushi prowess. Conversely, it's never too late to take a more than keen interest in food; life is too short to eat tastelessly. Becoming a Better Foodie should surely an irresistible lifetime commitment, but never taken too seriously.

This book is pink and chocolate, conjuring up delectable thoughts of freshly peeled, plump langoustines and hot chocolate fondant of deep intensity and single-plantation integrity. It is bulging with information to emulate not only my figure, but my insatiable appetite for Better Foodie knowledge: the in-depth, the exotic, the arcane and, call me fickle, the latest.

Do you want to be a Better Foodie?
how to acquire full gastro-credentials

Do you want to become the very best and wittiest, worldly-wise kind of unapologetic Foodie? Our self-avowed route to self-fulfilment is through eating with integrity, bettering our already demanding palate, and feeding our insatiable craving for culinary knowledge...and discovering the absolutely best place to buy a perfect macaroon.

AN ESSENTIAL PRE-REQUISITE is to have a more than reasonable appetite for excess without being indiscriminately greedy – in other words: an innate capacity for epicurean self-indulgence. Of course, not all Foodies are committed cooks (but they usually go that way), initially their foodism may merely extend to fulsome appreciation.

FOOD SHOPPING IS NOT A CHORE, especially when it involves beguiling specialist shops with great character and even better gastro-booty, and the mere scent of a food market is almost akin to setting a well-trained hound on a truffle trail. Our bookshelves are proudly crammed with iconic culinary bibles and our kitchens full of hard-core kit.

'I WON'T SEE THE DESSERT MENU; I'LL JUST HAVE AN ESPRESSO.' Although Better Foodies will rarely be heard to utter this, we'd rather have a modest feast of the very finest, than a gargantuan gorge of mediocrity. Every mealtime is precious, and we shamelessly plan the next, even whilst still salivating over our fresh pink-speckled borlotti bean, buffalo mozzarella and ripe fig salad drizzled with Taggiasca extra-virgin olive oil. We talk about food a lot – at least as much as many drool over their latest lover.

WE FULLY-FUNCTIONING FOODIES LIKE TO REMAIN ONE STEP AHEAD. We're the kind who check any listing of best places in the world to eat just to satisfy ourselves that we've visited at least half of the recommendations. We get an adrenaline rush every time we sit down expectantly at a restaurant table or plan a feast for friends.

OUR FOODIE MANTRAS are: provenance, seasonality, artisanal and single-estate, and we consider such impeccable credentials a necessity, not a luxury.

What kind of Foodie are you?

Who can resist a quiz? Are you a soft-core gastronaut who might not know a mandarin from a mandoline, yet are more than eager to learn, or a hardcore gastronome dedicated to expanding your culinary boundaries and eager to debate the finer differences between tataki and ceviche?

1. How often do you think about food a day?
A Rarely; you're preoccupied with more esoteric matters
B Almost constantly and definitely in-between meals
C Only when your tummy rumbles

2. How do you choose your holiday destinations?
A The loveliness of the beach – though a seaside shack selling chargrilled tentacle-twirling squid is a bonus
B By their proximity to hallowed food markets and iconic restaurants
C The lure of as much food as you can eat does it for you

3. What's your idea of a serious shopping day out?
A A day food shopping is a day wasted, who needs to touch, smell and salivate when it can all be done via the Internet
B A dawn-raid on your local farmers' market in preparation for supper, a mercy dash across town to the Iranian grocery for breads and spices, a rout around a specialist food bookshop and an hour or so of mentally, at least, up-grading your kit in a gleaming kitchenware shop
C Clothes, shoes, DVDs, lunch-on-the-go in a farmers' market and a quick dash into a chi-chi traiteur for supper

4. What are you most likely to dream of?

A Being holed up with a luscious Hollywood star

B A huge steaming plate of linguini dripping with white truffle, with the rest of the truffle and grater casually left on the table to help yourself

C A Champagne breakfast in bed, even if the croissants have been reheated

5. How do you like to celebrate your birthday?

A As usual at your favourite local gastro-restaurant, though you have a sneaky suspicion you've had the seabass with lobster tortellini three years in a row now

B You like to be surprised by dinner at a wondrous new off-the-celebrity-circuit discovery with a menu full of arcane, yet delectable delicacies

C You'll settle for nothing less than the full three Michelin star experience, preferably with more than a nod to Adria-ism

6. What does thinking seasonally mean to you?

A Time to consider up-grading the people carrier – the neighbours have the identical model and the top-of-the-range has far more room for the weekly food shop

B Eagerly anticipating the first of the season's wet walnuts and damsons

C It can only mean the fashion catwalk collections and another diet

7. What works for you to relieve tension and stress?

A Long country walks – but only if there's a fair chance of scooping up some delicious wild mushrooms

B Making a feel-good minestrone, preferably with some wonderfully fresh borlotti beans

C Eating a large bar of the highest cocoa percentage chocolate you can lay your hands on in one sitting

8. How far would you travel for a decent loaf of bread?

A The celebrity chef 'hand-baked' bread at your local supermarket stands up to the hype

B Distance is no object when a good crust and toothsome texture are at stake, and you'll purchase a stash for the freezer to justify the journey

C No distance; you were given a bread-maker and you actually still use it

9. How do you prefer your cheese?

A Delicate and not too pongy

B Pulsatingly strong or oozing seductively, definitely unpasturised and preferably very young or well-matured

C You're a pushover when it comes to sherry-rubbed rind manchego and vine leaf-wrapped goat's cheese

10. When was the last time you experienced liquid nitrogen?

A In chemistry lessons at school

B As a savoury meringue *amuse* when you finally secured a table at Heston Blumenthal's The Fat Duck

C What's that doing in a Foodie quiz? Is it something to do with those alchemist chefs?

11. What's your bedside reading?

A A thriller called *Juiced* with a rather explicit picture of a blood orange on the cover, a gripping read of Sicilian mafia exploits and culinary accidents

B The latest Foodie memoir by one of your all-time culinary icons – after sacrificing lunch (almost unheard of) to queue for a dedicated copy, you're hoping it will inspire you to write your own similar oeuvre

C An ever growing stack of lasciviously illustrated cookbooks, containing both favourite recipes and those you drool over, but would never actually attempt

12. Who are you most likely to confide in on a weekly basis?
A Your masseur/therapist
B Your local butcher who always saves veal bones for you
C Your best friend

13. What's your understanding of eating more adventurously?
A Splashing out on the latest celebrity chef regional-Indian-for-the-supermarket ready-meal with the enticing packaging
B Making a point, once a month, of buying an ingredient you have never cooked before and finding a recipe for it
C Drizzling truffle oil lavishly over your habitual repertoire

MOSTLY As: FRANKLY YOU ARE SCARCELY ON THE FOODIE RADAR. YOU PROBABLY INTEND THIS AS A GIFT, BUT YOU JUST MIGHT DEVELOP CRAVINGS FOR SOURDOUGH AND FONDUTA

MOSTLY Bs: YOU'RE A NEAR ENOUGH PERFECT SCRUMMY FOODIE, LIABLE TO DISPLAY PAROXYSMS OF PLEASURE AT A MERE SIGHTING OF SEA URCHIN ROE OR SHISO CRESS – JUST BE CAREFUL TO KEEP A SENSE OF PROPORTION AND HUMOUR ABOUT YOUR FASTIDIOUS DEDICATION TO CULINARY NIRVANA

MOSTLY Cs: YOU'RE FAST BECOMING A FLUENT FOODIE, BUT BEWARE OF THE FAUX FOODIE HYPE

GETTING started

How to be truly greedy without appearing so
and develop gustatory stamina

It's a delicate balance of satisfying unrepentant gourmet cravings and the urge to pick, however decorously, whilst keeping face – especially among those who don't quite share your unerring gustatory passion or in situations where you judge it's, sadly, simply inappropriate to contemplate thirds. On the quiet, away from do-gooder 'I can only manage a starter' types and whilst others train for marathons, we Better Foodies work on taste-bud flexing tactics for better tackling dégustation menus, purloining the last rosemary roastie and securing extra orange blossom water-infused buffalo ricotta ice-cream with dessert.

AT HOME ALWAYS SERVE YOURSELF LAST – that way it's easier to surreptitiously slide an extra goose-fat roast Maris Piper under your pheasant. The utterly shameless might deliberately 'forget' the pork belly crackling and bring it out separately when other guests are already busily tucking in and appear to divvy it up fairly.

OF COURSE IT'S ESSENTIAL and absolutely acceptable among fellow Foodies to insist guests start straight away as no-one wants half-cold culinary pleasure.

WHEN ANGLING FOR SECONDS, even if other guests are feigning fullness, comment fulsomely on how difficult it is to find samphire these days, how clever to think of matching zander with star anise, or how wonderful it is to enjoy caramelised quince at the height of its short season. Flattery will get you a fuller stomach! Or play the Foodie fanatic: whilst complimenting the dish mutter, about not being quite sure you detect the Chinese five-spice powder/yuzu (a tiny yellow Japanese citrus fruit with a limey zing). Your host should be flattered into offering you more without you appearing to be soliciting for seconds.

WHEN AT A DINNER PARTY AND THE CHEESE APPEARS, simply engage everyone in riveting, preferably non-cheese focused conversation, and slyly make cheese in roads every time you gesticulate a point. Note, however: it's likely that other guests may adopt similar tactics with their favoured cheese.

THOUGH THE CURRENT FASHION FOR SHARING MENUS might appear the solution, beware: portions are almost invariably too stingy for truly greedy sharing.

WHEN DINING OUT, DELIBERATE AND AGONISE OVER THE MENU to such an extent that your companions subliminally feel duty bound to plump for your also-ran choices – having established, of course, that it's strictly a sharing meal. Then inquire solicitously and effusively after everyone else's dishes and stick your fork in, but make sure you've practically finished your own scrupulously selected dish first.

WHEN YOU END UP SHARING, DON'T PLAY COMPLETELY FAIR. A well-timed bon mot along the lines of: 'I can't quite get how the tamarind fits into this dish and I really want to try it at home' works a treat. Or be more blatant: 'I've never tried this before (however unlikely that may be), it's so extraordinary. I simply can't resist just one more taste...'

WHEN FACED WITH AN IRRESISTIBLE CHEESEBOARD of oozing and pungent delights, ask so many impressively technical questions about raw milk, wheys and washed rinds that the self-styled cheese sommelier will warm to the theme. Delighted to expound to a fellow aficionado, you'll soon find samples of almost everything on your plate.

ARRIVE AT FARMERS' MARKETS, READY ARMED with your own supply of plastic spoons to facilitate sampling and avoid the worst of the unseemly scrum. When you find a particularly choice, recherché ingredient, engage the producer in informed, animated, ego-massaging chat, whilst you politely and repeatedly investigate the wagyu beef carpaccio.

RELIEVE YOUR FRANTICALLY-FROTHING WANNABE-ESPUMA-HOST and offer to serve out the Seville orange and ricotta tart, omitting to mention that pie charts were a bit of a weakness at school – the perfect excuse for helping yourself to an unfairly large slice of the cake.

Always offer to help clear plates

It's not really shameful to swipe that forlorn
last mouthful of salsa verde (pungent anchovy,
caper and herb) dextrously with your little finger
or rescue a stray *fraise des bois* (a tiny wild strawberry of
delirious intensity) that a fellow guest has inexplicably
left on the plate. There's the chance, too, of choice
pickings: perhaps the crispy rare breed bacon, which
has served its purpose embracing the mallard breast,
swiped straight from the roasting tray or a
surreptitious teaspoon dipped in the scrapings
of a glossy mustard sauce which didn't
quite make it to the table.

The Better Foodie store cupboard
definitive epicurean essentials

The quintessential litmus test for the Better Foodie is a highly considered store cupboard of definitive epicurean essentials for enjoying every meal to its utmost. It's never bare, far from it... Minimalism and the ferociously Foodie are wilfully incompatible. It's akin to investing in a wardrobe of classics. Why compromise the simplest spaghetti al limone with inferior pasta or eat vanilla ice cream without Madagascan vanilla pod seeds?

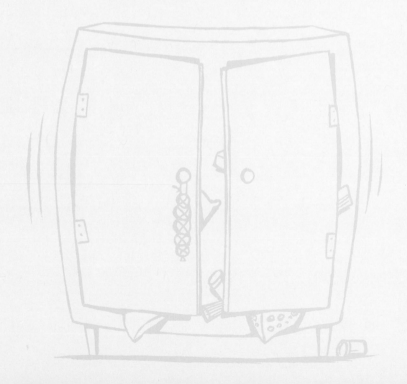

Better Foodies adore beans Tarbais from southwest France; haricot beans for cassoulet; dried or tinned borlotti; cannellini beans and chickpeas. And it's worth paying a bit more for jars of the plumpest Spanish beans.

Lentils Mottled teal Puy lentils; tiny, brown Castelluccio with a nutty, earthy flavour from Umbria; Black Beluga; Ustica (tiny and needing no prior soaking, these are cultivated entirely by hand).

Pearl barley (farro) Makes a good alternative risotto – for those Arnold Wesker moments.

More unusual grains Couscous; bulgar wheat for making tabbouleh; quinoa (pronounced keenwah) – both Charlie Trotter and Alain Ducasse are fans – and freekah, made from roasting young green wheat to give it a rich, smoky nutty taste – favoured in Middle Eastern dishes.

Top-quality dry pasta Even the best-intentioned Better Foodie doesn't always have time to make fresh pasta and knows that top-quality artisan dry pasta can be just as good. It's a question of paying a little more for a reputable name and looking out for slow-dried, where possible bronze die cut, durum wheat or egg pastas. Definitive spaghetti makes for good eating simply served *aglio olio*, with extra-virgin olive oil, garlic and chilli. For variety, offer chitarra, shaped after guitar strings, as a change from classic spaghetti. Keep penne rigate, too, with ridged quills to better hold the sauce, and a wide-ribboned papparadelle for chunkier sauces.

Flour Double 00, the finest grade Italian flour with exceptional elasticity for pasta, pizza and bread is non-negotiable. Alternatives like chestnut and chickpea or gram flour (for pakora) are useful stand-bys, too.

Better Foodies are rather smug about their rice collection

Arborio High starch content with plump grains – perfect for classic Milanese saffron risotto (de rigeur with osso buco).

Carnaroli from Po Large translucent grains with a white nutty centre. Uncompromisingly extravagant Foodies choose Ferron carnaroli with its distinctive blue paper mini sacks, made in Verona since 1650.

Vialone A shorter, fatter, rounder grain for a more soupy risotto and better suited to seafood and fish.

Calasparra Revered Spanish paella rice authentically used for Murcian caldero – rather like a risotto but made with a rich fish stock, enriched with tomatoes, garlic and blackened noras peppers and aïoli. Choose the bomba variety, which is plumper and has a better texture.

Basmati rice Must be the 'true line' traditional variety, rather than a hybrid. To the trained eye, the difference in size is perceptible. 'Pure' basmati has a milkier, nuttier fragrance, the grains remain more pleasingly separate and lengthen to almost twice their size when cooked.

Japanese ojiya Adventurous Foodies seek out this moist, silky soft rice.

Noodles Soba noodles for reviving broths; dried rice and glass noodles for Pad Thai or salads.

Roasted piquillo peppers An essential Better Foodie instant antipasto.

Tinned tomatoes San Marzano from Campania, preserved in their own juices, are the best; a jar of passata (sieved chopped tomatoes for almost instant sauces/pizza toppings); plus mi-cuit tomatoes – moister, juicier and richer in flavour than once ubiquitous sun-dried.

Panko Japanese coarse breadcrumbs made from slightly sweetened bread. They absorb little oil, giving a lighter, crisper finish to deep-fried squid.

Anchovies Though Italian-besotted Foodies swear allegiance to those salted and packed in jars, Ortiz, in their distinctive yellow and red retro tins, are truly the benchmark. Processed traditionally by hand within hours of being pulled from the Cantabrian sea, they are layered in salt for a day, rinsed, re-packed in salt and cured for five months. Dedicated Foodies are enamoured of smoked anchovies from Ramon Bue, too.

Capers Packed in sea salt to bring out their true flavour. Drowning a caper in vinegar is as unthinkable as overcooking pasta.

Canned tuna Defining quality is Ventresca di Bonito (an oil-rich pale pink under-belly fillet of exquisite delicacy) perfect on sourdough toast for supper.

Sardines The plumpest and best are Connetable from Brittany – the oldest cannery in the world. Fanatical Foodies splash out on 'vintage' sardines d'argent, fished at the end of summer, which improve with age.

Better Foodies simply don't do humble condiments

Salt

Though they do keep table salt for baking a turbot or roasting a salt-crust pineapple, their preference is for natural sea salt flakes, with a distinctive gentle texture and taste, or ivory fleur de sel de Guérande, hand-harvested from salt marshes on the Brittany coast (violet fleur de sel gives a delectable edge to the richest chocolate cake). Hungry for new taste experiences the Better Foodie yearns to add to their collection: coarser French sel gris marin with seaweed, for moreish foccacia; Himalayan pink salt brought down the mountains by yaks; Australian Murray River pink salt flakes; vibrant orange Hawaiian Red Alaea sea salt (its colour from red volcanic clay washed into the sea); Japanese gomashio or sesame salt for sprinking over soba noodles or rice; and ultra-rare, pricey oshima, harvested in the deep waters off the Japanese mainland and dried in solar greenhouses in bespoke ceramic jars.

Pepper

Once experienced, the incomparable sweet pungency of hand-picked unsprayed Wynad's Parameswaran black peppercorns from Kerala are the sine qua non. The Better Foodie also likes mildly aromatic Malaysian Sarawak and, when a more heady perfumed aroma is called for, Javanese long pepper. Arch Foodies fascinated by historical recipes may search in vain for grains of paradise. A good substitute is Szechuan pepper, known in Mandarin Chinese as 'flower pepper', from berries of prickly ash bush, with delicate nuances of anise and lemony overtones. Buy whole and roast in a dry non-stick pan until slightly smoking and crush. Modish, too, is Japanese sansho pepper with a piquant, haunting citrus flavour. Foodies with a taste for fiery pungency favour Tasmanian wild mountain or bush pepper – used sparingly, it gives an intoxicating warm inner glow to the tastebuds.

'A gourmet who thinks of calories is like a tart who looks at her watch.'

**James Beard, gourmet and founder of the eponymous
James Beard Foundation.**

Nam pla A Thai fish sauce that adds savoury unami flavour to casseroles, soups and sauces as well as Thai-inspired dishes. The best are fermented with anchovies fished from the Gulf of Thailand.

Mirin A sweet Japanese cooking wine that is used as a dipping sauce and in dressings.

Soy sauce or Japanese shoyu Contains wheat as well as soya, naturally brewed with no added colour or flavour.

White miso paste Mild/sweet fermented soya bean and rice, with salt added – an essential in miso soup and wondrous with grilled fish.

Bonito flakes Though Better Foodies always make their own stock they draw the line at Japanese dashi and, besides konbu (a variety of kelp that grows in the cold seas off the coast of North Japan), keep a supply of steamed, dried, smoked, cured and shaved bonito flakes. Only wipe, never wash or leave in boiling water, as the flavour lies on the surface.

Verjuice Unfermented grape juice. Better producers stipulate the grape variety. Verjuice has the tartness of lemon juice and the acidity of vinegar, though it is less harsh than either – delectable as a deglaze, dressing or dessert syrup.

Saba A cooked unfermented grape syrup that adds depth to classic bolognaise, soups and roasted root vegetables.

Rosewater and Orange Flower water Bought from an Iranian grocer – the supermarket essences are far too sweet.

Ume-shu A sweet/sour Japanese plum wine.

Pomegranate molasses Buy an authentic brand of this Middle Eastern staple. Its sweet/sour astringency transforms a chickpea, spinach, red onion and orange salad. Of course, the fanatical Better Foodie makes their own, according to Claudia Roden's recipe.

100 per cent pure Canadian maple syrup Each mature tree only produces 3.5 litres of sap a year and 40 litres are needed to produce just one litre of syrup – hence its price tag!

Honey No longer merely a choice between runny or set single variety/monofloral. Acacia is pale and mild; Greek, dark and almost as thick as treacle with pine notes; also hedgerow and borage. Rich amber Manuka honey from New Zealand is a must, not only on account of its aroma and rich taste but because it offers good digestive maintenance – essential for the committed Foodie!

Spice necessities Cardamom, coriander and the Better Foodie favourite: intense and complexly nuanced, sweet, bosky star anise. Bought whole as far as possible, ground and roasted freshly on demand, the proper Foodie likes to keep a stock of rarities as proof of their culinary rovings and sophisticated palate. Dried herbs are absolute anathema.

Chermoula A heady robust mix of cumin, coriander and sweet spices with lemon and garlic, which adds swoosh to grilled chicken and fish.

Baharat Arabic spice-mix with black pepper, cassia bark, cinnamon and nutmeg for long slow braises or barbecued seafood.

Slick oils to be proud of

KEEP THOSE CORE INGREDIENTS OF IRREFUTABLE QUALITY IN PRIME CONDITION. Tempting though it is to flaunt and drool over designer single estate extra-virgin olive oils collected on your culinary travels, they're best stored out of sight in cool, dark conditions. It makes good sense to buy a tin of intense, fruity, early harvest Arbequina cold-pressed, unfiltered olive oil each season and gradually decant it.

WHAT'S MORE, TOP-QUALITY OILS ARE WASTED on an impromptu frittata of newly in season violet artichokes or roasted root vegetables. Choose a good sunflower oil or a modish alternative – hemp, pumpkin, bran rice or cold-pressed rapeseed oil. Their higher smoke point means they can be heated to very high temperatures and won't cloud or solidify when chilled, so work well in dressings and marinades.

KEEP AVOCADO OIL ON WOK STAND-BY and walnut oil or, more recherché still, pistachio oil for special salads; pine nut oil, unsurprisingly, is superb for making pesto; French prune kernel oil with a hint of toasted almond is the latest addition for dressings and adds that extra je ne sais quoi to enrich pastry.

TROPHY EXTRA-VIRGIN OLIVE OILS that Better Foodies should try include: Spanish Nunez de Prado Flor (a free-flow juice with an incredible concentration of citrus and tropical fruit) and Gaziello's taggliasche Ligurian olive oil.

Ras Al Hanout Translates literally as 'top of the shop'. It is a legendary North African spice mix with numerous ingredients (anything from fifteen to more than one hundred) – including nutmeg, cinnamon, anise, cloves, cardamom, peppercorns, rose buds and ginger. Provides a Moroccan hit to tagines, cooked pulses, soups and roasts.

Jordanian Zatar A heady mix of thyme and toasted sesame seeds, often mixed with sumac and olive oil and brushed on flatbreads or on fish before grilling.

Peperoncino Hot red pepper flakes used in Sicily instead of black pepper.

Egyptian Dukkah A blend of roasted hazlenuts with strong aromatics and toasted sesame seeds – the perfect Foodie will grind their own. Dip good bread first into olive oil and then dukkah for pre-supper grazing.

Shichimi togarashi An edgy Japanese seven-spice mix of dried red chilli pepper flakes, sansho Japanese pepper, roasted, dried mandarin orange peel, hemp seeds, nori flakes, white sesame seeds and ginger.

Preserved lemons or limes A Moroccan staple. Preserving in salt adds complex spicy undertones to the sourness of the fruit. Only use the rind and discard the flesh. Adds piquancy to tagines, grilled fish and salads.

Sumac A crushed sourish berry, which richly partners roasted tomatoes.

Hot chilli jellies Intense with the sweet warm swoosh of Jamaican chilli pepper. Much imitated, Jules and Sharpie's hot pepper jellies are the Better Foodie's benchmark.

Red harissa A Fiery Moroccan chilli paste that gives depth to soups and stews and can be used as an accompaniment to couscous and tagines. The committed Foodie likes to make their own green harissa with fresh coriander, green chilli, garlic and aromatics.

Saffron Musky, slightly woody, exotic orangey-red filaments made from the hand-picked and dried stamen of violet crocus flowers. Only ever buy strands, not powder, and the richer and darker the better. Spanish and Italian are good; Kashmiri is best of all.

Mace The net membrane from harvested nutmeg – gives subtle fragrance to fish, stuffings and fruitcakes.

Maille Dijon mustard An everyday essential for dressings, Welsh rarebit, sauces and steaks.

Vanilla Buy only pure, slightly viscous Madagascan vanilla extract, perfumed and complex – never mind its expense. Long, slender dark brown vanilla pods are constantly replenished. Their tell-tale tiny black flecks trailed through custards and ice-creams confer elite epicurean status.

Fruit cheeses Useful for raising the game during spontaneous bread and cheese entertaining. Besides quince (aka membrillo) – symbiotic with manchego – try fig with goat and sheep's cheeses, pear with creamy blue cheeses, and plum with aged cheddar.

Biscuits Roka cheese biscuits; Poilâne biscuits for those impromptu, deserved coffee breaks; and Baratti & Milano (top Torinese coffee house) soft amaretti.

Vinegars for every occasion

Balsamic vinegar This has suffered from its uber-fashionable status. Better Foodies know balsamics are not created equal and spurn cheap pretenders fresh from factories, sweetened, thickened and coloured with caramel – however deceptively chic their bottle.

Aceto balsamico di Modena Made from boiled grape juice and vinegar and aged for at least three years. Reduce to a glaze to drizzle over roasted vegetables and salads.

Tradizionale (DOP) A wondrously complex syrupy elixir made from grape juice that has been fermented and passed through progressively smaller barrels made from mulberry, chestnut, juniper and ash over a minimum of 25 years, always reducing and concentrating. Used sparingly by select drop (chefs often use a pipette) it elevates a well-aged Parmigiano Reggiano or peak perfection strawberries to formidable Foodie nirvana.

Raspberry vinegar Although this may suffer from an *Abigail's Party* stigma, the more whimsical Womersley fruit vinegars – mostly from heritage fruits grown in the producer's Elizabethan walled garden – retain their Foodie standing.

Sherry and Cabernet Sauvignon vinegar Used profligately by Better Foodies who are also investigating the newest Spanish Cava vinegars.

Prada for the larder
rarified, hard-to-track-down extravagances

Even when the shelves are crammed to groaning with definitive epicurean essentials, the fanatical Better Foodie has to stay in the culinary fast lane. They cannot resist splurging on Prada for the larder for ingredients to transport a meal to a higher plane: whether a rarely sighted monofloral honey from Le Marche or a stash of piment d'esplette (Spanish pimenton of the highest order), a mostarda di frutta only made in Venezia, the latest recondite chilli or yet another obscure heritage fruit vinegar.

Armando Manni's cult Tuscan boutique-estate extra-virgin olive oil Produced from ultra-rare 500-year-old olivastra seggianese olives. So expensive, it is only sold in tiny bottles. Chef Giorgio Locatelli offers it only if he thinks a customer will properly appreciate it.

Artisanal jams Preferably those with a quirky story. Fortnum & Mason's floral, yet spicy rose petal jam and TeaTogether (former film-makers based in an atelier in Northern France who supply Ducasse and hip hoteliers worldwide), makers of poetic seasonal conserves: cherry; mirabelle with mead; greengage with walnuts; pear with cardamom; and star anise.

A tin of duck confit Ideally bought from a genial artisan duck producer after an hour or so of drinking floc in their Gascon kitchen on your last Foodie foray to southwest France. Deeply cynical, I was won over by La Ferme de Gagnet's confit... recommended by Joanne Harris no less.

A tin of goose fat Sourced from a highly reputable producer this imparts flavour to roasted Maris Piper potatoes like nothing else.

Robert Wilson twist-rolled Darjeeling From India (Himalayan) this retains the fragrance of newly mown grass, even in a teabag, transforming a restorative cuppa into an elixir – well worth its dizzying price.

L'Artisan du chocolat flakes For truly memorable hot chocolate.

Foodie trophies Jars of handmade fruit relishes/jams from Michelin starry establishments such as Michel Guérard's Les Prés D'Eugénie or Raymond Blanc's Le Manoir Aux Quat Saisons, which boast of recent culinary adventures.

The Better Foodie's cooking kit
essential gastro accessories without which a Better Foodie feels culinarily undressed

The kitchen and its accoutrements are the true benchmark of one's Foodie standing. Though we pride ourselves on being far from precious we're not averse to a liberal dash of sourcing one-upmanship, whether it's a wire dumpling scoop bartered from a street stall in Vietnam, the latest KitchenAid gadget or a cheffy espuma siphon.

WHAT DISTINGUISHES THE BETTER FOODIE FROM A MERE HOBBYIST is actually using the choice items of kit we so enjoy collecting. After all, working with exactly the right tools increases the pleasure of cooking immeasurably. Almost every shopping trip, especially on our culinary travels, includes feeding our extravagant appetite for kitchen emporia. We find caressing a sycamore chopping board or fondling a monumental granite pestle and mortar as satisfying as others find the most luxurious cashmere jumper or gleaming Harley Davidson.

WHILST IT'S EASY TO SCORN CELEBRITY CHEF MONIKER KITS, we judge on impeccable performance. Take Marco Pierre White's 'White Heat Collection', developed with venerable manufacturer Beka: the 1003 sauté pan has spot-on heat distribution for the ultimate omelette Arnold Bennett. Other names to conjure with include knives by Wusthof Dreizack (Raymond Blanc) and Mac (Thomas Keller, Heston Blumenthal and Nobu Matsuhisa). Of course, canny Foodies by-pass tempting yet chi-chi kitchen shops and trade-up to shop at professional chef stores such as Hansens.

BETTER FOODIES ARE RATHER SNOOTY ABOUT GARLIC CRUSHERS, as we know it is better to crush the clove with a smidgen of sea salt to release flavour more gently. We're equally iffy about bread-makers (although we must have a baking stone to ensure good crusts on our loaves and a wicker dough-proving basket), not to mention gimmicky gadgets such as mango pitters. We do, though, see the point of a 'spider' – a meshed spoon for serving pasta; so much better than pouring starchy water back over al dente pasta by sloppily tipping it all into a colander. And let's assume no Foodie would ever succumb to a chocolate fountain, even with a lifetime supply of best Valrhona Manjari. A bain-marie (makeshift or real McCoy) or fondue can perform a similar function for those who must.

What matters most are some good knives

RATHER THAN A DIFFERENT BLADE FOR EVERY CONCEIVABLE PURPOSE, the Better Foodie invests in a few of the very best: a 13cm cook's knife, a small paring knife, a serrated vegetable knife, an ultra-sharp toed and flexible boning knife for fish, and a carving knife – Better Foodies do not have a flesh-tearing electric carving knife.

THEY'VE PROBABLY TAKEN A KNIFE SKILL COURSE – Divertimenti and Leith's are good.

THEY WILL ALSO KNOW THAT THE STAINLESS STEEL/CARBON – from which a good knife blade is forged – should run all the way through the full length of the handle, for maximum strength.

WHILST NOT QUITE BESPOKE, the knife should feel the correct weight and balance for its user's hand. Favourites are ice-tempered razor sharp Global, Henkel, Wusthof, Dreizack and, for ergonomic perfection, Mac.

BETTER FOODIES WILL ALSO WANT TO TRY the newest sleekly professional Japanese Kai knives created in collaboration with Michel Bras.

A MATCHING SET IN A WOODEN BLOCK IS TOTALLY NON-FOODIE, and will blunt knives almost as badly as slinging them in a drawer. The Better Foodie likes knife magnet strips, especially cute circular Eva Solo ones. It is essential to keep covetable blades sharpened and honed to the finely pitched correct edge and angle with a sharpening steel.

FOR ADDED KUDOS, they casually refer to the 'Rockwell rating' of their knives: 56-8 and above is absolutely cutting edge.

I'M NOT WITH JOHN BETJAMAN WHO TOOK A SNOBBISHLY DIM VIEW OF FISH KNIVES, as mine are beautifully engraved and belonged to my grandmother. Besides, the smartest fiercely Foodie restaurants are investing anew in fish knives. Laguiole knives with matching fish forks are highly desirable and surely essential when enjoying fish on the bone.

LIKEWISE, I RECENTLY NOTED RAYMOND BLANC ADMIRINGLY AND APPROVINGLY FINGERING THE LAGUIOLE STEAK KNIVES at a degustation lunch at Heston Blumenthal's The Fat Duck. Such details add Better Foodie appropriate reverence to savouring a 21-day aged rib of rare breed beef. It's worth acknowledging that Laguiole knives were originally shepherd's pocket-knives. Ensure the knives are the genuine article; Claude Dozorme is a highly regarded craftsman.

THE PROPER FOODIE IS NOT CONTENT WITH JUST ONE CHEESE KNIFE – a dedicated parmesan knife, a scoop for Vacherin, a raclette slicer, stilton spoon and more are the kind of extras that make the committed Foodie content.

A plethora of recondite and vintage batterie de cuisine

Elizabeth David's culinary possessions
reached astonishing prices at auction. A
wooden coconut grater, a heavy-duty Indian
grinding stone for spices and a treasured beaten
silver bowl are the kind of souvenirs Better Foodies
like to bring back from their culinary travels. Sir
Terence Conran has Proustian vintage madeleine tins
in his London apartment. Rose Gray has a square
frame with wires stretched across it purely for cutting
the thinnest slices of puntarelle (an Italian chicory),
which she found totally irresistible while at an Italian
brocante. I hanker after full-on Foodie kitchen art to
join the mesmerising Malaysian food market
photographs given to me as a wedding present
by an arch Foodie photographer friend.

Top-quality, heavy-based, capacious saucepans, which conduct heat evenly, with snug-fitting lids and comfortable handles. Names to conjure with are: Calphalon, Circulon, Beka and All-Clad. Beware cheaper light, thin copper pans, which are liable to burn on the sides. Pans with an aluminium or copper core sandwiched between stainless steel running up the sides of the pan are good. Top of the fixated Foodie's wish list is, of course, a full set of Mauviel copper pans – nothing beats copper for heating and cooling quickly and evenly, giving more control. An amenable compromise is Mauviel's Cuprinox range – copper pans with stainless steel interiors and handles. Unlike traditional copper pans they don't need to be re-lined and can be used with metal utensils.

A weighty well-crafted casserole Le Creuset (French for crucible) – name-checked by Elizabeth David – are reassuringly labour-intensive in their manufacture and heat-retaining properties – perfect for oxtail and bitter chocolate daube.

A preserving pan, preferably copper for even heat distribution for making membrillo, jams and chutneys, is de rigeur.

A bamboo steamer So much better than a metal steamer. As Better Foodies know, the bamboo absorbs the water vapour, whereas water vapour condenses on the inside of a metal lid and back onto the vegetables, dissipating both flavour and vitamins.

Griddles Besides owning a heavy-duty ridged griddle for cooking meat and fish, Better Foodies should also have a dedicated griddle for crumpets and oatcakes and likewise a crêpe pan…and would like another one specifically for blinis.

A heat diffuser Often overlooked, this is a must for delicate sauces, as is a stainless steel splatter screen to use when sizzling pancetta or making tempura – it protects the stove from hot oil whilst allowing steam to escape.

Pressure-cookers Coveting one may sound prosaic and old-fashioned, but Heston Blumenthal swears by his for making all-important stocks of delectable concentrated finesse, quickly. At the other extreme, a slow-cooker is useful for out-all-day working Better Foodies. A greeting waft of slow-cooked Bowland lamb hotpot or organic chicken and Medjool date tagine does wonders for the stressed out gastronome's morale. We also like to have a dedicated tall stock-pot and a couscoussier.

Potato ricer The Better Foodie also needs one of these (an old-fashioned vegetable mill with a 25cm diameter is fine) for truly unctuous pomme purée to emulate Joel Robuchon's ambrosial mash, and an ultra-sharp, hand-held Japanese mandoline for occasional show-off cheffy flourishes.

Gorgeous chopping boards Despite the controversy a few years back, it's now accepted that hardwood is far better than plastic, as it naturally inhibits bacteria. The consummate Foodie veritably drools over ultra-desirable boards in London's Notting Hill's kitchen emporia, Summerfield & Bishop, or top-of-the-range David Mellor numbers.

A marble pastry-making slab, built into their kitchen, is a must for Better Foodies. If they are unfortunate enough not to have one, they'll want a Fernanda Italian wooden pastry board or a marble equivalent.

Chinois An ultra-fine mesh sieve for the truly dedicated stock-maker. It removes the small fat particles, which can result in bitter, insipid stock.

Gaggia coffee machine Ideally we'd all have a Gaggia coffee machine, which self-corrects the all-important water pressure. Its precision pump-operated system is far superior to a hissy steam machine, liable to scorch the coffee grounds. In practice, it's equally acceptable to use a stove-top espresso maker. The steam method forces water through coffee grounds under high pressure, making for dense aromatic coffee with an admirable rich crema – assuming the finely ground and roasted arabica beans are single plantation to start with. What's more: a simple aerolatte makes fulsomely frothy cappuccino (better still with skimmed milk) and doubles up as an apprentice espuma for those El Bulli foams.

Pestle and mortars The Better Foodie is enthralled by these and has several sizes – preferably made of granite or marble. Wooden ones look beautiful, but prove rather soft for pounding spices.

A Battery-operated digital probe Used to test meat temperatures, especially when cooking at fashionably low temperatures for unbelievably tender and juicy roasts (70°C for wonderfully aromatic seven-hour leg of lamb). However top-of-the-range the Better Foodie's oven is, they know it is best to have an oven thermometer at the ready to be absolutely precise.

Electronic scales These may smack of kitchen chemistry, but give the precision required when following more cheffy recipes.

Magimix Of course, the Better Foodie has a food processer, though a Bamix hand-held blender has the edge over a food processor (its whirling blades are smaller and rotate faster) for making soups and emulsions with a velvety-smooth texture. The electric spice grinder is much employed, as is the pasta-rolling machine and, of course, the Kitchen Aid mixer.

A wish list for fanatical Foodies

the trophy batterie de cuisine that the kitchen savvy, tempted-to-go-pro, Better Foodie covets

Better Foodies have to remind themselves they are not running a deli (though they often indulge in deli-running daydreams), nor a professional kitchen, but still they hanker after, and inevitably succumb to, many of those gastro-accessories that make life more appetising, including, in no particular order:

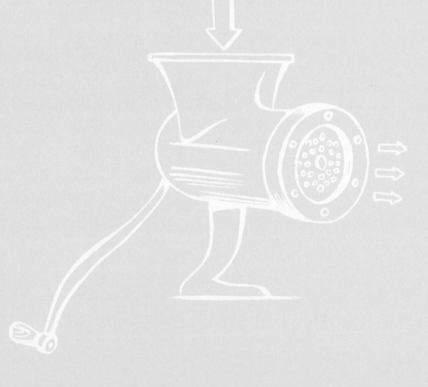

Retro hand-operated, heavy-duty mincers So handy for preparing rare breed mince for a smart shepherd's pie or peerless beefburgers. Useful for making sausages, too.

A copper cassoulette by Alessi With iconic designer provenance.

Mauviel's conical copper (tin-lined) hot chocolate stove-top pot Make sure you use L'Artisan du Chocolat flakes.

A rice colander and a sturdy skimmer For dishing up Persian rice and removing the tahdeeg (the irresistible crispy bottom of the rice).

Iranian-made electric rice cooker Recommended by the doyenne of Persian cuisine, Margaret Shaida, for foolproof rice. Or the more difficult-to-source desirables: a hagama (a traditional Japanese rice cooker) and a donabe (a Japanese ceramic pot for warming rice).

An old-fashioned Italian meat slicer

A pacojet The most longed-for modish gadget among truly aspirant Foodies. It opens up realms of possibilities for making ices instantaneously, purely from fruit or vegetables.

An espuma or thermo whip Cheffy though it is, for High Foodie Wow Factor one of these is wholly desirable. They resemble a soda siphon and cartridges of liquid nitrogen are added to 'charge' them. They are then injected into the liquid ingredients in the siphon and proceed to foam dramatically – perfect for home El Bulli style deconstructions, or more simply for adding a little chorizo froth to the butternut squash soup.

A Mauviel copper egg-beating bowl An object of both beauty and practicality.

Granite baking stone For simulating a traditional baker's brick oven to achieve that all important crust. An offcut from a reclamation yard is perfect.

A built-in coffee maker that grinds fresh beans for each cup For the kind of three Michelin star treatment Gordon Ramsay expects at home (Miele is the make to hanker after).

Handi pots from India Stainless steel lined insulated copper to use as serving dishes.

Dehydrator cabinets All the rage in New York for air-drying slices of fruit and vegetables without their losing their structure.

Vacuum marinators A pump removes the air and reduces marinating time from hours to minutes – so handy for black miso cod or spiced, marinated, slow-braised oxtail.

Rösle truffle slicer Wishful thinking perhaps…a specially ridged slicer for nonchalantly shaving those ultra-thin slices of Alba white truffle.

A smoker Don't settle for a cheap smoking mat as the resulting stench renders food inedible. Stainless steel Brooks smokers (developed for by-the-riverbank-fish-smoking for anglers) are heated with a fuel burner, rather than oil or charcoal, whilst Woodman smokers can be used on both hobs and barbecues. Most Better Foodies, however, simply fashion their own with a grill and rack, varying the smoke with pine needle, cigars or even vine clippings.

'*There is no love sincerer than the love of food.*'

George Bernard Shaw, playwright and Arch-Better Foodie.

What is the main ingredient in hummus?

Chickpeas.

How do you sweat vegetables?

Cook in oil over a gentle heat until soft and the juices are concentrated in the cooking fat. It's best to start with the saucepan lid on and take it off to allow the vegetables to caramelise slightly.

What is passata?

Pulped and steamed tomatoes, typically sold in bottles. An acceptable Better Foodie shortcut.

Is Cullen Skink a derogatory word for a poor cook or a kind of soup?

A traditional soup from the fishing village of Cullen made with smoked haddock, unsmoked bacon, potato and cream.

What kind of fowl is Bombay Duck?

It's actually a north Indian fish dish.

Which magazine claims to have first coined the term 'Foodie' and when?

Harpers & Queen, 1984.

Culinarily speaking, what does wilting mean?

Usually appplied to leafy green vegetables with a high water content, such as ruby chard or spinach. They are placed in a hot, dry pan with a little butter and seasoning and cooked ultra-briefly.

What is Sussex pond pudding?

A suet pudding that has a whole lemon in the centre, which melts into a delicious sauce.

Should a proper Irish stew have carrots?

Purists say the addition of carrots is wrong and consider turnips, pearl barley et al nefarious additions, too. The true Irish stew should be limited to neck mutton chops, onions and potatoes.

What are scapes?

Stalks, particularly of garlic bulb.

AT HOME WITH
The Better Foodie

The Better Foodie househunter
location is all

Househunting is always deeply trying whatever the budget, but at least the Better Foodie is certain about the immutable gastro-criteria that necessarily dictate their preferred neighbourhoods and the pivotal importance of true kitchen potential within a likely property. When selling, the canny Better Foodie encourages mealtime viewings to tempt vendors with the gastro-good life.

CLOSE PROXIMITY TO A DROOL-INDUCING, ASTUTELY STOCKED DELI IS NON-NEGOTIABLE. Being within ambling-whilst-you-contemplate-a-seasonal-supper-distance to that rare trinity of butcher, baker and fishmonger and, let's be greedy, greengrocer too, is liable to induce furious bidding wars between Foodie househunters. Ideally, there should also be a regular farmers' market near enough for that spur-of-the-moment 'let's roast a porchetta' decision. A good local bistro is worth a premium – de luxe or unreconstructed rustic is irrelevant, as long as the chef truly cares – as is an Asian-inspired hot spot. A particularly fine Perigord salade tiède (it was the late eighties) dictated the location of our first house!

OF COURSE, THE ACTUAL HOME MATTERS, TOO – particularly the kitchen potential. It's not only a question of size, it should have the best and sunniest aspect of the property. After all this is where home Foodies spend most of their waking hours. And gazing out at the lovingly tended bucolic potager, beyond the purple basil and perilla on the south-facing windowsill, would be blissful. Plenty of space for a huge table is crucial, conducive to many, many hours of sociable cooking and Foodie banter. A proper cold larder and an unresurrected airing cupboard for proving dough and culturing yoghurt are far more desirable than a walk-in dressing room.

THE DINING AL FRESCO ALLURE OF THE GARDEN IS CRUCIAL – whether for a solitary crema espresso and cannoli (gorgeous Sicilian pastry tubes stuffed with fresh ricotta, dried fruit and chocolate) mid-morning, or a summer feast for eight. There should be capacity, too, for the aforementioned potager, or at least a container version. In a worst-case scenario an allotment in the neighbourhood – and the means fair or foul to jump the queue – will do. The more glutinous gardeners among us will covet an allotment to supplement domestic mizuna/scorzonera (black salsify) supplies.

A Better Foodie kitchen
the heat of the matter: the quintessential heart of the Better Foodie's raison d'être

The Better Foodie's kitchen is their haven, the epicentre of their copper mixing bowl (so much better for whisking) cravings. Whether unfitted with rustic, retro French/Scandinavian influences or ultra svelte, cutting edge contemporary – or even fully bespoke – it's beyond fashion. What matters is not only its hard-wearing, high performance, multi-tasking functionality, but its role as a place of extreme emotional importance and real beauty. It's where the Better Foodie can bask in the glory of sybaritic entertaining or simply spend many hours revelling in culinary mooching.

THE TRULY COMMITTED WILL HANKER AFTER A SECOND, STEAM OVEN, preferably a Gaggenau combi-oven – so useful for holding in moisture when making bread, pastries and cakes. Ideally it will come complete with a built-in temperature probe and baking stone, and perhaps a wood-burning oven. They know that chefs now rate induction-cooking hobs as the way forward (especially good for precision-control slow-simmering and chocolate-tempering) and long to add a customised Wolf cook top to their kitchen.

A BESPOKE LARDER IS THE DE TROP FOODIE'S EQUIVALENT OF A LOUIS VUITTON VANITY CASE, yet far more practical. It should be sited on an external north-facing wall with proper ventilation and feature marble or granite shelves for cheese and charcuterie, besides plenty of deep racking. Where space is at a premium, Smallbone's flying food cupboard or angled spice drawer insert are acceptable larder solutions. These will save you fumbling in the black hole back of a cupboard for lemon myrtle or star anise.

IT'S SCARCELY CONCEIVABLE TO HAVE TOO MUCH STORAGE. Besides a batterie of cupboards, think about an armoire, too, for displaying the most ravishing, tactile and eclectic tableware. There should be plenty of extra-deep drawers, which can take serious weight – for pans, including the fish kettle, over-sized serving platters et al. Plus plenty of shelves veritably bulging under the weight of well-thumbed be-splattered cookbooks.

A CAPACIOUS FRIDGE IS DE RIGEUR. The aspirant Foodie demands Sub Zero refrigerated drawers and stainless steel marinating bins, not to mention a built-in water filtering system, fulfilling a deep-rooted fantasy to run their own restaurant.

A trophy cooker...

...unlike a status gas-guzzling 4x4 car will not
depreciate in value. I've known a top-of-the-range
gleaming Falcon, Lacanche or Gaggenau to clinch a
house sale. The minimum six-burner stove should have
a flame that will go very high and very low (although
a heat-diffuser is always a viable option), an in built
griddle or, better still, a charcoal grill, and a high-power
wok burner, together with extra-wide double ovens
with ultra-low temperature options (for seven-
hour-braised salt marsh lamb).

THE FOODIE KITCHEN SHOULD IDEALLY CONTAIN TWO SINKS. One should be shallow, for food preparation – for soaking the puntarelle in iced water (necessary to make it open up and curl seductively) and draining the agnolotti pasta – and one for washing-up – deep enough for cleaning the stockpot/couscoussier. Their position is also key: one close to the stove is a good idea, preferably with a hose tap, making it possible to fill a pan while it sits on the hob, a filter system providing cold-filtered water and instant hot water.

THE HOLY GRAIL IS TO HAVE SUFFICIENT WORKSPACE FOR MUCH GREGARIOUS PREPARATION. Marble not only improves with patina but is perfect for pastry; Corian or stainless steel are timelessly durable, too. Well-lit worktops should be cannily planned – probably with a sociable, central island-unit within sight of the stove – so that it's easy to join in conversations whilst preparing, yet keep cooking mess hidden from view...who's ever heard of a fanatically tidy Foodie?

SPECIALIST EXTRACTION WITH SERIOUS, PROFESSIONAL POWER is unequivocally essential (Gaggenau or Miele lead the field). As most Better Foodies believe wholeheartedly in entertaining in the kitchen, they wisely choose to site the high-powered extraction motor on an external wall. Who wants to be reminded of an Arbroath smoky brunch when sitting down to a delicate supper of diver-caught scallops with white raisins and capers or have their high Foodie banter rudely punctuated with invasive whirring?

The Better Foodie garden
making the most of the intimate connection between plot and plate

It's more a case of licking fingers than green fingers for the Better Foodie, who views their outdoor room, whatever its proportions, as a passport to better eating...a veritable edible Eden. Thoughtful planning (apple varieties that ripen at different times) and planting (borlotti beans for height and colour, a quince standard for magnolia-like bossom and gorgeous, fragrant fruit) can transform even the most unprepossessing urban garden. For inside many of us beats the heart of a hopeful smallholder, growing not only for the sake of self-sufficiency, but for pure epicurean pleasure.

A POTAGER (PREFERRED TERMINOLOGY FOR VEGETABLE PLOT), even within the most unpromising terraced urban garden or roof terrace, is practically non-negotiable. It works admirably for River Café's Rose Gray, whose central London rooftop boasts bountiful basil varieties including purple and lemon, sweet marjoram for salmoriglio (crushed with sea salt and combined with olive oil/lemon juice it is the summery sauce for wild sea bass), cicore (a dandelion like winter chicory) and radicchio di Treviso.

IT'S TERRIBLY PLEASURABLE TO BE ABLE TO OFFER GUESTS AN AFTER DINNER HERB INFUSION IN HOMAGE TO MODERN – the new restaurant at New York's MOMA. There the waiter wheels a huge trolley – the kind that usually displays the cheese – abounding with a forest of mint, thyme and other greenery, which is freshly clipped into a chic teapot at the table for post-prandial tisanes.

FOR THE UNASSUMING METROPOLITAN GARDEN think in terms of unfussy edible plants which can be trained against a wall or trellis, such as tart redcurrants, the unmistakable musk-like aroma of quinces, pink-mottled, creamy, nutty borlotti and Lady of the Field green beans with their pretty pink striations. The height of gastronomy is to grow coco beans, which are consummately cheffy and absolutely not related to cacao beans.

THE LATEST TALK IS OF THE INFINITE POSSIBILITIES OF JAPANESE SALAD AND VEGETABLES: from fukim and red kabui to udo, red perilla, amaranth, sansho peppers and shungiku (edible Japanese chrysanthemums). Visit: www.namayasai.co.uk for further information. Foodies are also experimenting with cultivating mushrooms – from shitake to morel – on leaf moulds and grass cuttings on oak logs – so convenient for a Sunday supper of 'wild-ish' fungi risotto when there's no time to foray.

ALTHOUGH IT'S SATISFYING TO GROW THE EXPECTED BASICS, the Better Foodie cannot help but seek out the unusual and arcane, which only adds to the pleasure of matter-of-factly announcing that the sweet succulent pea shoots adorning the broad bean risotto are from the garden.

A CONSTANT HERB SUPPLY IS OBLIGATORY. Aside from everyday culinary essentials – chervil, dill, parsley, basil (as well as purple look out for lemon, cinnamon and chocolate basil – favourites for desserts, according to salad producer supremo Richard Vine, supplier to Gordon Ramsay et al) – the proper Foodie cultivates the old-fashioned wild herbs foraging chefs are so fond of: chickweed, sweet woodruff, sweet cicely, hyssop and salad burnet. Those supermarket pouches, which wilt on impact with the fridge, are a waste of space.

THE CHALLENGE IS GROWING FOODIE ESSENTIALS like fresh garlic; the quirky: padron peppers, perfect for impromptu tapas, simply fried in oil and scattered liberally with sea-salt; and the outrageously sought-after, such as barba di frate (similar to huge chives, slightly bitter, served braised with olive oil and garlic as a side dish, rather like samphire) and fraises des bois (heavenly fragrant tiny semi-wild strawberries). Better Foodie gardeners exchange cuttings and recipes among fellow plot-holders with the fervour many Foodies reserve for exchanging restaurant recommendations.

THE TRULY COMMITTED FOODIE WILL PLOT AND BRIBE TO SECURE AN ALLOTMENT, however unprepossessing its rough and ready beauty. The gluttonous gardener absolutely goes to town, planting from seed (perhaps joyfully misshapen Marmande tomatoes smuggled back from Gascony – the seeds left out to dry on the kitchen table)…where their eagerness for speedy edible results doesn't get the better of them.

Planting is strictly gastro-centric...

...planned purely with the intention of nourishing our insatiable appetite for eating with the seasons and furthering our culinary borders. Include in your plot a selection of edible flowers:

Peppery nasturium Vibrant with roasted scallops

Violets For exquisite homemade violet confit to accompany a grassy Spring goat's cheese salad; or make a floral sugar for exquisite meringues – crystallise the petals to use as decoration.

Lavender For butterflied leg of lamb with lavender and thyme flowers. A few lavender stalks added to the barbecue coals make for more fragrant cooking.

Jasmine Delicately cuts through the richness of a crème brûlée.

MICROCLIMATE ALLOWING, other Foodie desirables include: tomatoes (plum Perini and cherry); Sweet One Hundred (a much maligned, and now resurrected, butterhead lettuce), plus Romaine Mortarella (with subtle pink lacing) for Caesar salad; old-fashioned purslane and sorrel; cime di rapa (sprouting turnip tops); and, of course, the irrefutable rocket.

OUTDOOR COOKING NEEDS TO BE VERY CAREFULLY CONSIDERED. Better Foodies trade up to super-annulated, off-road techniques for more ambitious and inventive entertaining and barbecues, such as the Nipoori, which works rather like a domestic tandoori with skewers to plunge dukkah-crusted tuna into an almost instantaneous fire.

AS AN ADJUNCT TO THE BARBECUE, the committed Better Foodie may spend many hours musing over the logistics of digging an Imu fire hole (a Hawaiian custom) – wonderful for a juniper-spiked porchetta. More practically, consider building an outdoor traditional brick oven (unlike a kitchen extension there are no potential planning difficulties) to produce bread of deep aroma and definitive crust, not to mention the most tender pizza and Lebanese mechouri. Tom Jaine of Prospect Books has written the would-be wood-fired oven proprietor's bible. Still not convinced? Nobuyuki Matsuhisa had a wood-fired oven built in his garden solely for new-style Japanese entertaining at New Year.

LANDED FOODIES FORTUNATE ENOUGH TO HAVE THEIR OWN APPLE ORCHARDS prefer rare and vintage varieties like the sweet Beauty of Bath, juicy James Grieve or late-picking Laxton's Superb (a particular favourite at Brogdale, home of the UK's national fruit collection, where more than 2,300 varieties are cultivated). A wooden apple tray is an aesthetically pleasing and frost-free way to flaunt your bounty.

'*Great sorrow or great joy should bring intense hunger — not abstinence from food, as our novelists would have it.*'

Sir Arthur Conan Doyle, wit and nineteenth-century English author of Sherlock Holmes.

Even the birds fare rather well

Consider feathered gourmet needs, too. Perhaps a peanut cake or maybe some sunflower seeds, with the black husks removed to enable easy access to the nutrient-rich hearts without any beak straining. Foodies enjoy watching robin, finch and company pecking antics over a leisurely brioche (irresistible crumbs) breakfast.

COMPOST FIGURES LARGE in the lives of Better Foodie gardeners, who are given to paroxysms of pleasure at the effect of the peelings of their Belle de Fontenay potatoes on their early, lovingly nurtured fraises des bois.

HAVE FOODIETUDE AND THINK LONG-TERM APPETITE RETURN. Plant a low-maintenance tartufaio in the garden (a hazelbush whose roots are impregnated with truffle spores). Choose indigenous varieties, such as the prized, intensely perfumed bianchetto for a winter harvest or walnut-sized scorzone (also known as English truffle) for a summer harvest – and a perfect accompaniment to scrambled egg. Be realistic: White Alba will never proliferate beyond Piedmont. After four or five years the first truffles should grow and after 12 years a 100g harvest (no pig required) can be greedily anticipated, which puts the outrageously high price of wondrous truffle in perspective.

DEEP DOWN, WE URBAN FOODIES FANTASISE ABOUT A RURAL ARCADIA WHERE WE'D BE VIRTUALLY SELF-SUFFICIENT; it's a soothing diversion when negotiating the rush hour to meditate on growing our own cardoons – essential for dipping in bagna cauda – and pulling up our own Ratte (Joel Robuchon's preferred potato for his legendary pomme purée). We may even drool over seed catalogues, mentally planning serried rows of cavolo nero, mulberry bushes for jams, and the planting of fig, medlar, damson, pear and apple trees.

MOST IMPORTANTLY, CAREFUL CONSIDERATION SHOULD BE GIVEN TO THE POSITIONING OF THE TABLE for maximum fragrant wafts of appetite-whetting, still-on-the-vine San Marzano tomatoes and Italian rosemary. Eating alfresco is greedily relished and Better Foodies maximise on outdoor entertaining possibilities.

Better Foodie parents and children
how to ensure the Better-Foodie-in-training child eats their purple sprouting broccoli

Better Foodies are at their most righteous when it comes to practising gastro-parenting. It starts, of course, in the womb, with nurturing the unborn Better-Foodie-in-the-making's tastebuds by eating even more impeccably seasonally, organically and discerningly than ever. Such solicitous pre-natal preparation is an ideal excuse for a pre-baby pilgrimage to a long-aspired-to iconic restaurant and makes the perfect, if perhaps premature, initiation into a lifetime of supreme good eating.

THE PREGNANT BETTER FOODIE has read all the latest research on how the culinary sensibilities of the unborn child are formed. They diligently ensure the Better-Foodie-to-be is exposed to a wide-ranging sophisticated Foodie palate. The pregnant Better Foodie probably continues to eat raw milk cheeses – as long as she's confident in their provenance – but reluctantly passes on the foie gras and venison liver.

AMONG THE BETTER-FOODIE-TO-BE'S FIRST PRESENTS (Better Foodie god-parents, please note) should be an exquisite set of cutlery for making pleasurable light work of those all-important first morsels. Initially, the budding-Better-Foodie-baby is lovingly prepared seasonal purées from winter squash to avocado and jersey royal, graduating to proper grissini, risottos and fishcakes.

THE CULINARILY-RAISED INFANT will doubtless have visited their first restaurant well before they're six months old. I remember requesting a table for three at a notable fish restaurant in St Ives, Cornwall, when my son was barely past four months. Although he spent most of it contentedly snoozing under the table, it may subliminally explain why he's developed such a penchant for langoustines!

THE PROPER FOODIE BELIEVES IN TEACHING BY EXAMPLE that food is important and should be treated with respect and interest, if not rapt delight, from the earliest age. They start the habit of eating together as a family whilst still at the purée stage. Better Foodies encourage their children to be curious about food, to ask lots of questions (and will provide plain-speaking explanations of where food comes from), they introduce Foodie mantras, such as seasonality, sustainability and organic early on and, equally importantly, encourage them to be eager to try new foods.

BETTER FOODIE CHILDREN WILL QUICKLY DEVELOP A PRECOCIOUS ABILITY WITH CHOPSTICKS as dim sum – lots of sharing and plenty of buzz as new dishes constantly arrive – is a favourite among Better Foodie families.

THE BETTER FOODIE CHILD WILL SOON BE ABLE TO REEL OFF THE NAMES OF AS MANY CHEFS AS FOOTBALLERS OR POPSTARS and will probably have experienced their food, too. They'll also know that three Michelin stars is even better than getting an A* in Maths. Beware, however: they may start initiating their own must-have Foodie experiences list at a tender age. My eleven year-old Better Foodie son, Theo, quite rightly insisted the only way to celebrate his grandma's 70th birthday was with a full-blown tea party at The Ritz!

HOW BETTER TO INSTIL AN EARLY LOVE OF VEGETABLES than light-hearted instruction in peeling, podding fresh peas and, better still, picking vegetables and fruit. A favourite Better Foodie family day out is a visit to the local pick-your-own farm, whatever the season. It's rare for a formative Foodie child to refuse a boiled egg with hand-selected first-of-the-season asparagus soldiers or hedgerow blackberry and apple crumble.

ANOTHER FAVOURITE BETTER FOODIE FAMILY OUTING IS TO A FARMERS' MARKET, where trainee Better Foodies are encouraged to taste and help select ingredients. The lure of freshly made falafel is enough to make my son eager to spend Saturday mornings at Borough market and he always persuades me to buy far more cheese than I intend to. Locally, too, he's more likely to implore me to stop off for some pecorino or Somerset Rambler at our neighbourhood cheese shop, Hamish Johnson, than pester for pick n' mix at the corner shop.

The formative Better Foodie child...

...always has friends clamouring for sleepover
invitations, as their proper Foodie parents believe
in pulling out the stops with suitably enticing
edible treats including:

Bomboloni Italian mini doughnuts filled with ricotta.

Homemade ice cream With Canestrelli
(artisan thick wafers sandwiched with dark chocolate
and hazelnut gianduja) to accompany a movie.

Homemade blueberry muffins
In readiness for a midnight feast.

An indulgent breakfast Freshly griddled pancakes
with rare-breed crispy bacon and maple syrup plus
homemade smoothie cocktails.

The Better Foodie child must do vegetables

and their parents must do their utmost not to
be caught feeding them mangetout in the winter;
vegetables should be strictly seasonal and produced
locally as far as possible. Ditto fruit – though I admit
my son became rather partial to physallis early on and,
even now, occasionally has them in his lunchbox.
The Better Foodie child probably takes a packed lunch
to school and no one scoffs at my son's regular Baltic
rye bread sandwich of Montgomery Cheddar or
smoked salmon, plus vegetable crudités and an
English apple. Occasionally, there's a square
of Valrhona chocolate as a treat.

ALTHOUGH THE BETTER FOODIE PARENT IS NOT COMPLETELY SANCTIMONIOUS, THERE ARE CERTAIN LIMITS. Fast-food restaurants are not considered treats; they are only resorted to in extreme emergencies, if at all, and are preferably off-limits – bar decent fish and chips and sushi.

AT BIRTHDAY PARTIES, the Better Foodie child absolutely always has to have a homemade cake of impeccable organic ingredients, creatively decorated. Own-made cheese stars (courtesy of Nigella's recipe) are de rigeur. Homemade popcorn also goes down a treat at parties and should always be taken to the cinema, too.

OF COURSE, ALMOST ALL CHILDREN ARE PASTAVORES and will soon learn to recognise the better brands of durum wheat dried pasta when time is too precious to make your own – the formative Foodie child learns how to work a pasta machine around the same time as they learn to ride a bike. Better still, they'll appreciate that different shapes suit different sauces and will happily ring the changes with spelt pasta, too. And, as a special treat, they adore fresh spinach and ricotta ravioli from a proper Italian deli – scattered with the herbs that they've grown themselves, of course.

INTRODUCING THE FORMATIVE FOODIE CHILD TO GOOD CHOCOLATE OF IMPECCABLE PROVENANCE IS ESSENTIAL. Organise a chocolate tasting for their friends – they will really appreciate the subtle nuances of red fruit and leather – or implore the newly formed Academy of Chocolate to visit their school. The Better Foodie parent doesn't consider it wantonly extravagant to give their child a L'Artisan du Chocolat Easter egg; their child will appreciate it isn't only size that matters and will notice any furtive parental attacks on the shell!

THE BETTER FOODIE PARENT BELIEVES IN STARTING THE COOKBOOK HABIT YOUNG – a sure-fire way of enticing Better Foodie children to suggest their own menus. I still vividly recall working my way though *The Learn to Cook Book* longing to get to the baked Alaska. As a child of ten or so, one of my favourite Sunday afternoon treats was curling up with an enticing selection of cookery books at more Foodie relatives' homes and avidly scribbling down inspiration in my recipe notebook!

IT'S HARD TO AVOID BECOMING A COMPETITIVE BETTER FOODIE PARENT – especially when it comes to harvest festival and school fête cake stalls. As a seasoned cake stall holder, I take an extremely dim view of any parent who tries to sneak in a non-homemade offering and note appreciatively those whose baking is outstanding – perhaps even as prospective new friends! Of course, the Better Foodie parent is as proud of their formative Foodie's culinary milestones as of their academic prowess, and can't help boasting – just a little – of evidence of their progeny's adventurous and already well-defined palate.

Teaching their child to cook using proper, fresh ingredients...

...is taken at least as seriously as the more usual parental concerns of encouraging piano playing and swimming lessons. The Better Foodie parent shudders at the thought of cookie kits full of unforgivable extraneous 'nasties', and would rather not do funny-face pizzas. Instead, they make soda bread (children love kneading); minestrone (plenty of opportunity for knife-craft); roast organic chicken (initiating them in the joys of the chicken oyster attached to the backbone – the Better Foodie's understanding of chicken nugget! Foodie children instinctively suck on the bones, too); authentic hummus, and proper trifle. They'll probably even have a go at Heston Blumenthal's recipe for homemade tomato ketchup and will prefer to make their own baked beans.

The Better Foodie library

how to feed the mind and join the linguine literatti

For those of us who dedicate an extra-large portion of our lives to our insatiable appetite for food knowledge, it's axiomatic that we have an all-consuming penchant for purchasing books: irresistibly appealing with their indefinite shelf life and opportunities for vicarious eating.

A Better Foodie's books are always unapologetically well-thumbed, more than a little sticky and jus-besplattered, and rarely bought only for one recipe.

Our collection extends beyond groaning shelves, packed tighter than the best-salted capers in the kitchen. In our fantasies, like Nigella, we have our own two-storey dedicated voluptuous library, but in reality, compelling recent purchases are stacked in inviting piles around the house. By the bed we have a veritable croque-en-bouche (statuesque profiterole confection favoured at French weddings) of culinary escapism: a mix of soothing pre-snooze tomes (perhaps favourite Elizabeth David or Claudia Roden volumes) and, for indulging in a midnight feast of fantasising, a choice volume penned by a 'pin-up Foodie' such as Marc Veyrat or Thomas Keller, whose restaurants are so dizzyingly expensive and hard-to-book that we simply enjoy being evocatively transported to a virtual dinner.

We're liable to become evangelical about our favourite authors to the point where we'd be happy just to see their shopping lists. At worst we have an irritating (to feeble Foodies) habit of reading out nuggets of arcane history and provenance like over-excited children. Excruciating though it sounds, we can't help but pre-judge other Foodie's credentials by a scan of the book jackets on their shelves before supper.

We've already appropriated the book club – we meet to dissect and salivate over the latest, defining gastro tome and each cook a sample dish for a profoundly satisfying supper. Likewise, we're highly approving of the more erudite chefs/restaurateurs who've instigated book soirées at their restaurants – such as raconteur-to-be-relished Jeremy Lee of the Blueprint Café above London's Design Museum.

WE'RE FASCINATED BY THE FANATICAL FOCUS OF SINGLE
SUBJECT COOKBOOKS – with more than everything you needed to know
about vanilla, cod or mustard.

WE'RE VORACIOUS GASTRO-MAGAZINE SUBSCRIBERS, TOO.
The satisfying thud of *Gourmet, Saveur, Gourmet Traveller, Delicious, Olive, Vogue
Entertaining* or New Zealand's *Cuisine* on the doormat is almost as thrilling
as winning the lottery and dinner at New York's Jean-Georges. Those of us
with an extreme habit of intellectual nourishment will let slip that we have
a standing order for *Petit Propos Culinaire* – the thrice-yearly, semi-academic
periodical started by the late Alan Davidson and perpetuated by Tom Jaine
of Prospect Books, dedicated to the history of food. We also subscribe to
Gastronomica, a cutting edge American title focused on historical, literary and
cultural food scholarship.

BETTER FOODIES ARE MORE THAN TEMPTED TO AMASS
ANTIQUARIAN COOKBOOKS. This remains one of the few buoyant
markets in the antique business and the Better Foodie takes pride in having
a hotline to out-of-print guru Liz Seeber for esoteric and rare desirables.

COOKERY BOOKSHOPS, OF COURSE, EXERCISE AN INEXORABLE
GRAVITATIONAL PULL ON BETTER FOODIES, who long to be on first
name terms with owners of seminal stores including Books for Cooks in
London's Notting Hill and its namesake in Victoria and Sydney, Australia;
and Kitchen Arts and Letters, on Lexington Avenue, New York.

THE ACCOLADES THAT MATTER to us in terms of culinary clout are
the André Simon, Glenfiddich, James Beard, the British Guild of Food
Writers and World Gourmand awards.

A Foodie's literary taste will combine the complementary flavours of:

The Scholarly The paradigm of culinary knowledge is Alan Davidson's phenomenally researched, yet readable, *The Oxford Companion to Food*.

The Cerebral Harold McGee's *On Food & Cooking: The Science and Lore of the Kitchen* – Heston credits it as an indispensable swot book!

Classics Including the high literary priestess of Mediterranean cuisine Patience Gray's exquisite oeuvre, *Honey from a Weed*.

The Practical The best-friend-for-every-occasion-chattiness of Simon Hopkinson's *Roast Chicken and Other Stories*.

The Better Foodie's wardrobe

dressing to disguise and stylishly accommodate gustatory greed

For many of us Better Foodies, our shape bears witness to how much we embrace food with passion, purpose and style. But we still aspire to be as well-dressed as the definitive mizuna leaf salad. We seek out well-sculpted clothes, which skim greedy curves, and favour forgiving, flowing pleats (Issay Miyake is our muse) over belly-pronouncing sharp tailoring. Clinched waists and tucked in shirts are anathemas and, always mindful of the next good meal, we wear our discreetly elasticised, appetite-friendly apparel with hedonistic abandon.

WE'VE ALMOST DEFINITELY TRANSCENDED OUR PHASE OF
WEARING NUTMEG GRATER AND WHISK EARRINGS/CUFFLINKS.
I confess that I once succumbed to a cocoa bean pendant – a forgivable
gesture, perhaps, as it was specially commissioned by Torinese gianduiotti
chocolate guru Gobino. We are, however, rather partial to sartorial
purchases to remind of us of a culinary epiphany: the spangle-spiralled
earrings that recall the first tasting of Parisian Pierre Hermé's wondrous
patisserie, or the genuine Breton beret purchased after a particularly
memorable cotriade (a wondrous fish stew).

APING ECCENTRIC FOODIE FASHIONISTA QUIRKS – Marc Veyrat's
penchant for nineteenth-century parson's head attire for example – should
be avoided. Aspiring to a Brioni suit like the one Heston Blumenthal is
invariably seen in for award-ceremonies is, however, to be applauded.

WE'RE APPROVING, TOO, OF THOSE DESIGNERS WHO SHARE
OUR FOODIE FANATICISM and are more inclined to yearn for their
labels. We nod knowingly about shoe designer Emma Hope's penchant for
classic crème brûlée, Paul Costelloe's craving for native oysters, and share
handbag designer Lulu Guinness's appreciation of the perfect simplicity of
good tempura or sushi.

THE BETTER FOODIE ESCHEWS FASHION-VICTIM MICRO-
HANDBAGS in favour of more capaciously styled receptacles – it's
accessorising in anticipation. We're bound to beg a restaurant menu in
order to re-enact a hallowed meal, whilst purloining any last remaining
morsels of sublime petits fours for our Better Foodie children. And we need
to be able to carry, with panache, those irresistible impromptu Prada for the
larder purchases.

The Better Foodie pet
why a rare breed Middle White piglet makes a Better Foodie best friend

Pets in the conventional sense don't figure largely on the Better Foodie's gastrometer of domestic priorities. There are those who insist on calling their pooches Truffle (presumably regardless of the limited opportunities to prove their tuber-foraging prowess) and their cats Galangal (as a precious and more tangy alternative to ginger).

COUNT YOUR CHICKENS — preferably of the rarer breed Cotswold Legbar variety — and gloat about how their fabulous yellow yolks are on a par with their Italian corn-fed counterparts. Keeping fowl has never been so fashionable, especially since the debut of the Eglu (www.omlet.co.uk), the ultimate in funky chicken housing, with room for four organically reared chickens, stylish wooden flooring and an innovative 'eggport' for egg collection. Gathering warm eggs from one's own chickens has to rate as one of life's best simple luxuries. Quails are quietly gaining favour, too, with fiendishly fiddly fried quails eggs being the mark of a modish warm salad.

BEE KEEPING HAS AN ENDEARING, ALBEIT COMPETITIVE, BUZZ. Once, it was enough to serve melodic honey from the hives of the Paris Opera House roof. Now, it's more foodcentrically acceptable to have one's own hives — on the roof of your apartment — and appreciate the nuances of different honey varietals with the reverence once reserved for extra-virgin olive oil. Bee husbandry classes are thriving among Foodie urbanites. It is smugly explained that city bees tend to produce more and better honey than those in the countryside, due to the near constant booty of eclectic nectar to be harvested from parks, gardens and window boxes; in the countryside, bees may be limited to a single crop that flowers once a year.

REAR A RARE BREED PIGGY WEANER (an already weaned growing pig, requiring only a modest porcine ark and exercise terrace). Gloucester Old Spot, Middle Whites and flop-eared British Lops are favoured swine. Foodies slaver at the thought of inviting friends to sample their own bacon, salami, hams, sausages and other charcuterie. The alternative is to 'adopt' a pig: pick a rare or endangered breed and have it brought up for you in a free-range environment. Visiting is permitted, it is slaughtered humanely and can be delivered to your door in customised cuts. (www.numberonepig.co.uk)

What salad favourite was once called 'love apple'?

Tomato.

What kind of milk is best for full froth cappucinos and why?

Skimmed milk. The proteins within the milk are adsorbed, which gives stability to the bubbles at the liquid's surface and creates a better class of froth. Milk froths better at lower temperatures, too.

How long have potatoes been around?

Around 2000 years. They were first cultivated by Indian Incas in what is now Peru, who developed over 1000 words to describe them!

What kind of fish roe should taramasalata authentically be made from?

Dried and salted grey mullet roe, but it is often made with more readily available smoked cod's roe.

What is in an omelette Arnold Bennett?

An omelette with smoked haddock and cream.

Which part of the pomegranate is inedible?
The white membrane separating the seeds into compartments
is incredibly tannic.

What are enoki, shiitake and puffball?
Mushrooms. Enoki are tiny Japanese mushrooms resembling a pale
brown porcupine; shiitake are Chinese, flattish and dark brown;
puffball are sizeable white spheres – found wild in British meadows –
delicious halved and grilled with butter, garlic and parsley.

**Which small ivory-coloured grain cooks like rice, but
more quickly, and was the staple food of the Incas?**
Quinoa.

**When and why did sausages become known as
bangers?**
During the food shortages of Second World War, they contained so
much water that they would often explode when cooking.

What is Scotch Woodcock?
Toast with anchovy paste, topped with scrambled egg.

HOW THE BETTER FOODIE
entertains

How the Better Foodie entertains
studied nonchalance is all

It's absoluely untrue (whatever dour social commentators may decry): dinner partying – even if it is referred to as supper in the kitchen – is vigorously alive and kicking (as vociferously as a Venetian moleche soft-shelled crab before it hits the pan) in Better Foodie circles. In fact, for many, it's the absolute highlight of the working week and the lifeblood of their social nexus. It's widely known that behind the scenes of studied thrown-together nonchalence, high-flying Better Foodies strategically schedule business meetings to dovetail surreptitious assignments with game dealers or forays to the best cheese affineur in town.

FOR MANY FOODIES, THE ANTICIPATION AND TRAWLING to the furthest reaches to track down the finest and most specialist Foodie gems is at least as pleasurable as the actual entertaining. We think nothing of a cross-metropolitan trek to procure the best smoked eel or Poilâne loaf – although we will make sure our guests realise the lengths we willingly go to.

WE LIKE TO FLAUNT OUR RELATIONSHIP WITH THE LOCAL BUTCHER/FISHMONGER (a prime consideration when we moved house) and serve something rather arcane – perhaps salt-marsh or heritage Southdown lamb – or something terribly P.C. – maybe an under rated, sustainably-fished species: megrim sole, red gurnard or recondite hake cheeks. We can't help but boast if we're fortunate enough to have an 'in' with a cheffy supplier: Wild Harvest for our fungi or my local pasta-maker, Vittorio Maschio, who makes pasta for Giorgio Locatelli (his pasta is still bronze die cut with a rougher finish to hold the sauce better).

IT'S TAKEN AS READ THAT BETTER FOODIE GUESTS WILL WANT TO KNOW THE PROVENANCE OF THEIR DINNER. New dinner party etiquette (emulating the most High Foodie restaurants) is to introduce dishes by name, where they're from and, where appropriate, who made them.

THE DINING TABLE MATTERS, but we're certainly not tempted by those precocious dress plates/chargers that the most de luxe establishments showily remove before any food arrives. We may well, however, choose tableware we've admired in a favourite restaurant. I admit my white porcelain Jasper Conran for Wedgwood plates are identical to those on which Giorgio Locatelli serves his sublime risotto. I'll also confess that in the deepest recesses of my Foodie past, I proudly bought those half moon vegetable plates that were all the rage in the 1980s.

One dish with wow factor is a well-honed wheeze

A cassoulet, tagine (served in the properly authentic terracotta tagine we lugged back from Marrakesh), bouillabaisse or salt-baked bream invariably elicits rapt enthusiasm from our appreciative guests. Details matter: strictly seasonal vegetables, creatively presented, are obligatory. Winning suggestions include a celeriac, swede and Roseval potato gratin, or broad beans (double de-podded, please) with fresh peas and their shoot tendrils. Salad is desirable, but no bags hastily decanted; a simple butterhead or escarole lettuce with a scattering of caperberries and chervil is much more pleasing.

WE DON'T LIKE TO HAVE HEADILY FRAGRANT FLOWERS on the table as they detract from enticing culinary aromas, (ditto, scented candles), though we may succumb to a row of small and perfectly formed pots of herbs, which wittily relate to the meal. A still life of arresting fruit is a good alternative (pomegranate and figs are a favourite) and a long thin white porcelain or wooden dish of clementines is also highly effective.

A FAVOURITE RUSE IS TO COMBINE DRINKS WITH A SHARING STARTER, ensuring the pre-dinner stage doesn't go on too long, risking the main course going past its prime. Dukkah, an earthy, fragrant Egyptian blend of dry-roasted and ground sesame, coriander, cumin, hazelnut and salt is winningly simple, yet different. Serve with warm flatbread dipped in olive oil. A good winter choice is bagna cauda, a warm Piedmontese anchovy, garlic, egg and olive oil dip, preferably prepared in the bespoke bagna cauda dish that you brought back from the last Slow Food Salone del Gusto in Turin (the ultimate epicurean market – mind-boggling in its scope and specialities). Serve with seasonal crudités – for absolute authenticity, procure some cardoons in their brief winter season.

BREAD IS TREATED SERIOUSLY. Ideally, we make our own fougasse, sourdough or dramatically extra-long breadsticks dipped in Maldon sea salt or, if we're hell-bent on impressing, have individual rolls personalised at Poilâne. We happily make the effort to have a special farmers' market butter or splash out on Lescure from Charente-Poitou.

NO DOUBT FOOD WILL BE THE MAIN TOPIC OF CONVERSATION, so provide some outrageously outré talking points: a Slow Food Presidia cheese, a heritage pear of impressive pedigree or a memento of your recent travels – maybe a slab of Sardinian bottarga to shave over the fish stew.

ENCOURAGE YOUR GUESTS TO MINGLE IN THE KITCHEN, and issue spontaneous invitations. This is a good opportunity to demonstrate our Better Foodie resourcefulness and well-stocked larder.

PROPER FOODIES ADORE CHEESE, especially those made with raw milk, traditional rennet and with interesting washed or blooming rinds. We try and limit ourselves to one or two beautiful cheeses of contrasting texture. Serve on a gorgeous tactile misshapen olive wood board with homemade membrillo (quince jelly) and good biscuits that properly complement the cheese. Perhaps with some fresh Medjool dates still on the stalk or peak perfection figs, too.

WE'RE CERTAINLY GREEDY ENOUGH TO DO DESSERT AS WELL – ALWAYS HOMEMADE. We're slightly sniffy about the French proclivity to buy in a tart, unless we have a patisserie of Pierre Hermé or William Curley stature in our neighbourhood. And we rather like finishing up with a named cru – single-plantation chocolate-tasting board, ultra-grown up artisan fruit jellies or a more unusual sweetmeat – candied Portuguese Elvas plums or soft, fresh diamond-shaped calissons if we've just returned from Aix-en-Provence (made from ground almonds, glacéed orange and melon peel and orange flower water, topped with icing sugar).

WITH THE SINGLE PLANTATION COFFEE we always have on stand-by La Perrouche unrefined roughly cut sugar cubes. The coffee should be served in rather precious espresso cups with vintage coffee spoons – though Slitti (a top-ranking Turin chocolatier) chocolate spoons coated with dark cocoa powder make for a decadent extra. As an alternative we like to offer real Moroccan mint tea (freshly snipped from the garden) in colourful Kasbah tea glasses.

We're not that competitive... really

Or we at least do our best to disguise it.
But we do like to exceed expectations and
live up to our gastrocentric credentials. Sometimes
we need to remind ourselves that we're not trying to
impress a restaurant inspector. We do have our
favourite dishes, but we're usually driven to expand
our culinary repertoire. We will confidently experiment
on our guests, especially if it involves a bit of behind-
the-scenes high calibre technique: a Gloucester
Old Spot pork and English rose veal terrine with
Iranian pistachios, perhaps casually presented for
DIY serving on a rather special David Mellor
sycamore chopping board, with an
accompanying bowl of cornichons.

Better Foodie table matters
why sitting comfortably is meal-enhancing

Let's face it: the Better Foodie is an unrepentant purist when it comes to table matters. This doesn't mean being a stickler for formal table settings and plans; the Better Foodie favours more relaxed dining with the emphasis on good eating rather than impeccable manners.

WHAT MATTERS IS A SIMPLE TABLE DRESSING to enhance rather than distract from the food. Crisp, understated napkins – linen tea towels picked up on Foodie travels (maybe from Dean & Delucca or Peck in Milan) work well. For full Foodie impact tie with raffia and place a cinnamon stick and star anise on each, to hint at flavours to follow.

KEEP EXTRANEOUS, NON-EDIBLE DECORATION TO A MINIMUM. Tiny tea glasses filled with delicately fragrant flowers are unexpectedly effective. Alternatively, perhaps try some edible nasturtiums, a selection of fresh herbs in tiny terracotta pots or artfully arranged seasonal fruit or vegetables – globe artichokes and purple-tinged baby turnips. All such table adornments are kept restrained and low – it's more relaxed and means guests can easily indulge in Foodie banter across the table.

PLATES SHOULD BE UNFUSSY, probably white, preferably tantalisingly tactile and none too precious – in keeping with the sensual emphasis on taste and visual appeal. Sophie Conran's first designs for Portmerrion may eclipse many a Better Foodie's loyalty to sibling Jasper Conran's Wedgwood, but a few whimsical, talking-point, vintage serving dishes don't go amiss. Remember: Better Foodie guests like to help themselves at the table – it allows them to be surreptitiously greedy and invariably provokes much animated deeply Foodie discussion about the preparation of each dish.

BETTER FOODIES WITH AN EYE FOR COLLECTABLE TABLEWARE should keep tabs on Tricia Guild of Designer's Guild, with her unerring judgement for spotting the most talented just-out-of-college, up-and-coming designers. They will also while away many pleasurable hours compiling mental wish-lists at contemporary global tableware specialist, Vessel, in London's Notting Hill.

Recherché accessories to enhance the pleasure of dining:

handmade sharkskin grater for fresh wasabi

vibrant glass platters via The Conran Shop

splendid gnarled olive wood cheeseboard elevated to an artwork

exquisitely simple porcelain rice bowls or sake cups by a fashionable Japanese ceramicist, such as Ryoko Nakano or Mizuyo Yamashita

serving platter by Tord Boontje

BETTER FOODIES LIKE TO FLAUNT THEIR CONDIMENTS: a coloured glass salt cellar to display the fleur de sel and a granite thumb-pot for the just crushed, lightly roasted Wynad peppercorns. Alternatively, matching Perfex retro-French brass salt and pepper mills. Very fortunate Foodies may have self-indulgently invested in a little table art – perhaps a hand-crafted, bronze Mark Brazier-Jones salt and pepper maze, complete with its own tiny spoons.

CUTLERY SHOULD BE NONE-TOO ORNATE (Alessi are good for understated contemporary polished stainless-steel) and glassware must sparkle: Riedel for wine, plus, for that quirky boho edge, William Yeoward water glasses.

FLATTERING LIGHTING IS ESSENTIAL. Celebrated restaurant designer David Collins insists that lighting is absolutely key to a happy dining room. An effective balance is achieved by some unselfconscious, elegant tea-lights or votives on the table, a restrained candelabra for a grander festive gesture – so long as it doesn't dominate the meal or conversation (use good quality high beeswax proportion candles to outlast the most expansive dinner) and adjustable downlighters elsewhere for maximum control.

ABOVE ALL, SEATING MUST BE METICULOUSLY CONSIDERED, and comfortable, as Better Foodies and their guests will invariably spend many, many hours around the table.

Unusual delicacies others ignore
but that Better Foodies devour

Never let it be said that the Better Foodie is recklessly extravagant. Far more (criollo bean and salted macadamia nut) brownie points are to be gained by proffering an erstwhile overlooked gastro-delicacy, however humble its origins. Fergus Henderson of London's St John restaurant, who created 'nose-to-tail-eating', has a lot to answer for. Topics of competitive gastro-conversation may include the correct way to cook chaps (pig's cheeks) and whether anyone has had the good fortune to try the subtle taste of slow-poached lamb tongues – ravishing with sauce gribiche (capers, cornichons, eggs, mustard, parsley, extra-virgin olive oil and vinegar).

Chicken oysters The sweet, almost juicy, darker morsel of flesh where the backbone and the base of the chicken thigh meet. French Foodies call this the sot-l'y laisse (stupid ones leave there!).

Duck scratchings Riding on the wave of rare breed, artisan-made pork scratchings and attracting cult Foodie nibbling status, rarely made duck scratchings deserve recognition, too.

Bones of Teruel and pata negra ham For memorable stocks of the utmost intensity.

Fish cheeks Monk, skate, halibut; even monk liver and the Spanish sauté cod tongue. Offal fiends are particularly partial to cod chitterlings, which taste rather like herring roe.

Hake throat The Basques call it kokotxas. It is even more of a delicacy than cheek and served in foodiecentric San Sebastian with pil-pil sauce.

Prawn shells After eating prawns, the Japanese fry the shells as tempura.

Prawn heads Nooror Steppe, chef-co-proprietor of Blue Elephant Thai restaurants, recommends that tom yam soup should be made with the insides of prawn heads for total authenticity.

Lobster claws Considered a delicacy to be sucked decorously in Tokyo, home of the most refined kaiseki Japanese dining.

Lobster coral With truly fabulous colour. Mash into butter; the flavour elevates simply grilled fish to ultra-gastro status.

Dripping

The fat that drips from a fore-rib, or other cut,
of beef into the roasting tin is a much under rated
gastronomic gem. Forget its associations with post-war
austerity and treat it as the British answer to Gascony's
goose fat – irresistible spread onto crusty toast with
sea salt, for definitive roasted vegetables or for
making the ultimate fat chips.

Courgette/zucchini flowers Delectable when stuffed with buffalo ricotta and then fried.

Beetroot leaves When roasting a fresh beetroot, keep the leaves to blanch and add to a salad, as the French do.

Radish leaves A dandelion alternative for sophisticated bitter salads, especially to accompany a young fresh goat's cheese. Customarily used in Northern France.

Garlic scapes The stalks of new season fresh garlic. Newly omnipresent in British revivalist cooking, though long used in Asian stir-fries.

Brussel tops No doubt inspired by the River Café intoxication with cime di rapa (turnip tops). These have far more interesting flavour than sprouts – and not just for Christmas.

Pumpkin seeds Roast with olive oil, sea salt and spice for healthy, thrifty nibbles.

Apricot kernels Crush into homemade apricot jam to add a subtle, almondy nuance.

Parmigiano Reggiano rind Gives unami intensity to stocks, especially when making vegetable risotto or minestrone.

Better Foodie recherché nibbles
why dry-roasted peanuts really won't do

It's really not flippant among Better Foodies to believe that first impressions do count – culinarily-speaking anyway. Hence the importance of suitably recherché nibbles. Attention to such details is the epicurean equivalent of being sartorially well-accessorised and go a long way to maintaining and enhancing all-important Better Foodie status. Of course, when a guest, the Better Foodie must be able to identify the most arcane recherché nibbles; it really isn't done to be caught less than fully gastro-aware.

IT'S SIMPLY NOT DONE TO OFFER SALTED PISTACHIOS, even if they are the plumpest finest Iranian examples – though Catalunya salted Marcona almonds (preferably grade 16, extra crispy and juicy) might pass muster, as would homemade sweet chilli pecans.

OLIVES ARE WHOLLY ACCEPTABLE if first-of-the-season intensely floral/herby Catalan Arbequina or freshly harvested, grassy, luscious Petit Lucques, from southwest France. With Portuguese Foodie comestibles increasingly representing the Mediterranean region to flaunt, Elvas olives, marinated in wild oregano from the same eastern Portuguese estate as the divine Elvas plum sweetmeats, hit the mark on the Foodie barometer.

IT IS FAR MORE GASTRO-CHIC to serve a sumptuous yet simple deli spread: an unctuous hunk of culatello, aged parmigicno reggiano to graze on and bowls of choice marinated artichokes, Pantelleria caperberries, roasted aubergine with pomegranate yoghurt dressing, cornichons et al.

A NOTE OF WARNING: Heaven forbid stooping to those discs in a tube, so beloved by budget airlines, or bought-in dips-in-a-tub.

Storecupboard recherché nibbles

Taralli A Puglian favourite. Savoury yeast dough enriched with egg-knot- or figure-of-eight-shaped biscuits that have been cooked twice. They are either baked twice, or boiled then baked. Often flavoured with fennel seeds.

Smoked Spanish anchovies and wood-roasted piquillo peppers The only morsel to serve on cocktail sticks.

Harissa roasted chick-peas or rosemary, cayenne and walnut oil roasted cobnuts.

Edamame beans (Frozen and ready podded are fine) with sea salt, chilli, rice wine vinegar and soy sauce.

Guindillas Sweet-pickled, green, massively moreish Spanish chillies.

A home-assembled variation on Western Indian bhel puri With puffed rice; sev (deep-fried chickpea flour noodles flavoured with chilli and fenugreek leaf), and tomato and cucumber in lime cumin and tamarind dressing. Serve with some natural Greek yoghurt and coriander in individual bowls with spoons.

Free-range quails eggs Dip into a homemade sea salt mix with grated lime zest or sansho (Japanese green pepper) or the Japanese condiment, furikake. Alternatively, smoked quail's eggs (a speciality of Inverawe smokehouse).

Complex spoonfuls and savoury lollipops...

...artfully arranged, are best left to the
high-end professional party caterers. The
Better Foodie doesn't want to be the one left in
the kitchen garnishing canapés. Whilst we like to
be cutting-edge, we're after instant wow factor with
the palate-provoking taste impact to match with
unexpected and diverting flavours. And we
certainly want to be invited back!

The savvy Better Foodie serves a signature amuse:

Dill or kumera (sweet potato) blini Serve with horseradish crème fraîche and home-cured salmon or, better still, recondite smoked carp.

Orzotto cakes Gently dribbling with truffled fontina.

Pistachio, chilli, yoghurt and chickpea flour kofte With a tamarind dipping sauce.

Warm salt-cod brandade with wakame (seaweed) crisps.

Diver-caught scallop (must be sushi fresh) ceviche On homemade fresh maize tortilla.

Sizzling hot, mini spicy chorizo Preferably partnered with oysters. Helford, Kumamoto or Blue Point are Better Foodie oyster preferences.

Brocciu (Corsican goat's cheese) gougères A puff pastry take on the cheese straw.

Paper-thin slices of cecina A dark red, intensely rich beef from Spain that has been salted, smoked over oak and cured for 18 months – more recherché than bresaola – accompanied by courgette caviar (barely blanched courgette, blended with crème fraîche and black pepper).

Venison liver terrine Intensely rich, topped with a caperberry. Or, if you have recently returned from Gascony and are feeling magnanimous, most Better Foodies pounce on mi-cuit foie gras.

Divine dips

Bagna cauda A hot anchovy, garlic and oil
Piedmontese dip. Fanatical Better Foodies
have a bespoke earthenware pot with a
flame solely for this 'hot bath'.

Bissara Moroccan broad bean.

Garlicky pistachio aillade
Authentically High Foodie with
grilled asparagus.

Muhammara
Aubergine and crushed walnut.

Sicilian lemony artichoke.

Nyons olive and orange tapenade
Particularly good with crisp radishes to dip.

Serve with flatbread, lacey lotus root crisps and
'heritage' vegetable crudités.

The more hands-on
the better

Pa amb Tomaquet Only if the tomatoes
(preferably Moneymaker, Cherokee Purple or sweet
100) are wondrously ripe, sweet and fruity. This is the
Spanish custom of drizzling olive oil and rubbing fresh
garlic and cut tomato into good crusty bread.

Flatbread to dip in extra virgin olive oil.
Preferably choose a talking-point oil –
perhaps Il Palagio from Trudie Styler and
Sting's Tuscan estate (only from Harrods)
and homemade dukkah.

Choice culatello or Joselito lomo – smoked
and cured acorn-fed Iberico pork coated in pimenton.
For guests to slice on a temptingly tactile wooden
board. Serve with cornichons; mild, crunchy, pickled
garlic and marinated and grilled baby violet artichokes.

Infinitely more stylish is to proffer a huge, gorgeous platter of a single, intricately-prepared morsel:

Vietnamese rice paper rolls Filled with lime and herb suffused North Atlantic prawns with a Nobu inspired dip.

Sustainably farmed or wild, line-caught salmon/tuna tataki Just-seared and immediately refreshed in iced water, cooled and then sliced ultra-thin and finally sprinkled with gomasio (a nutty-tasting, Japanese-style sesame salt).

'Shots' or 'shakes' of hot or cold soup To flaunt our current cheffy bedtime reading or parade a recent demi-tasse/tea-glass gem purchase. If we're in possession of such recherché kit, these shots should be foamed through an espuma.

Bottarga (Sardinian) or **Avgotaraho** (Greek) **Mullet roe** Shaved onto crostini of an earthy aubergine caponata.

Paper-thin slices of melt-in-the-mouth peppery Joselito iberico chorizo From free-ranging acorn-fed iberico pigs. Serve on romesco (pepper, tomato, almond mix) crostini.

Nonchalant Foodie gems
to throw into dinner party conversation

Whilst Better Foodies indubitably see each other so that they can have dinner – rather than dinner being an aside to social banter – good conversation (meaningfully translating as gastro-centric) immeasurably elevates the occasion. It's wise to have a few tasty bon mots prepared earlier to scatter liberally into the melée. Word spreads mellifluously within the Foodie inner dinner circuit: highly appreciative, gregarious Better Foodies with a switched-on line in recherché repartee find themselves much in favour and invited to all the most hedonistic epicurean occasions.

WHEN PROFFERING THE BUFFALO MOZZARELLA, BLACK CRIM TOMATO AND BASIL SALAD: Did you know that basil contains essential oils (namely estragol and eugenol), which help you to wind down in the evening? It's also rather good as a tisane alternative infusion to mint.

AS YOU HAND AROUND THE DIVER-CAUGHT SCALLOP SASHIMI: Did you know most so-called fragrant fresh wasabi is phoney? It's a mix of horseradish and mustard powder, coloured green. The wasabi plant (we eat the ground roots) grows wild only in cool shallow pools of ultra-pure water, often high in the mountains. According to Peter Gordon, the fusion finesse chef, New Zealand now cultivates it very successfully.

AS YOU PRODUCE THE HOMEMADE GRAVADLAKS (flavoured only with salt, sugar, dill and pepper and an accompanying sweet Dijon mustard sauce): Did you know the Scandinavian 'gravlaks' literally means buried salmon? Originally, it was actually buried for the cure – wrapped in birch bark, placed in a hole in the ground and covered with earth for several weeks until almost fermented!

DEFTLY TRANSFERRING THE BLUE LE CREUSET CASSEROLE of slow braised oxtail and szechuan spiced belly pork to the table: Did you know that Elizabeth David was responsible for Le Creuset introducing its cast-iron pans in blue – inspired by the colour of her ever present Gauloise?

SERVING UP THE BLACK COD, (elevated to cult status in the Nobu dish, and now available at the best fishmongers and The Fish Society) with white miso sauce, let slip that it is also known as sablefish and caught in Alaskan Pacific waters, and not in the least related to the cod family. Its exceptional flavour is due to its rich oil content.

PASSING THE DELICATELY DRESSED SALAD OF GREEN SHISO LEAVES (also known as perilla): Did you know that shiso are actually related to the mint family? The blue flowers, tasting faintly of cucumber, are borage from the garden, which are reputably terribly good at easing colds and sore throats.

PROFFERING THE VIOLET IMBUED SHORTBREAD to accompany blood orange and Pedro Ximenez pannacotta: Did you know violets are a herb and considered such a culinary delicacy in Toulouse that they have their own festival?

OF COURSE, GREEN AND BLACK OLIVES ARE THE SAME, BLACK ARE ONLY RIPER. This never fails to silence some doubting smart arse.

DID YOU KNOW THAT SOME CULTURES STILL CONSIDER IT THE HEIGHT OF RUDENESS TO TALK DURING DINNER? Sherpas spend several hours having animated discussions before dining in silence, and in traditional Iranian households it is good manners to talk before eating, too.

OF COURSE CAESAR SALAD HAS NOTHING TO DO WITH JULIUS CAESAR. It was created by an Italian restaurateur in Mexico in 1942, Caesar Cardini, who'd been hosting a group of Hollywood socialites during Prohibition, and had to whip up a store cupboard feast.

AS YOU SERVE UP COLCHESTER NATIVES WITH CHORIZO: Do you know how to distinguish native oysters from rock, even before tasting them? Natives are roughly fan-shaped with one half of the shell flat and the other cupped, whilst Pacific (sometimes known as gigas) are more deeply cupped, rougher and more elongated.

'One cannot think well, love well, sleep well, if one has not dined well.'

Virginia Woolf on 'The Importance of Eating'
in *A Room of One's Own*.

Have you tried the world's most expensive jam?

Confiture de groseilles, from Bar-le-Duc has been
the preserve of the rich and powerful since the Middle
Ages. Hitchcock had it flown to his film locations to
satisfy his breakfast jam fixation. Each hand-picked
redcurrant really is de-seeded with a quill.

HAVE YOU HEARD ABOUT THE CHEF IN CHICAGO who has devised a way of modifying printer heads to make edible menus using vegetable and fruit juices? The paper itself is made of soy bean and potato starch and printed sheets are dipped in a secret soy/sugar mix before baking.

DID YOU KNOW THE FIELDS USED FOR JERSEY ROYALS ARE USUALLY DRESSED WITH SEAWEED AS A FERTILISER? They're the only potato with Protected Designation of Origin status and, however many others I try, their waxy, delicate sweet earthy taste is incomparable.

HAVE YOU TRIED ROCK SAMPHIRE BEFORE? Though Shakespeare (in King Lear) considered samphire collectors the lowest of the low, I think it's great with fish, though of course it's only around in July and August.

SERVING UP HOME-MADE PUMPKIN RAVIOLI with crushed amaretti biscuits, nutmeg, sugar and a dollop of mostarda di frutta: Did you know that during the Renaissance, wealthy Florentines would show off by serving pasta with costly sugar and spices? Of course, I realise it's a dish that is traditionally served on Christmas Eve in Lombardy, but I had the mostarda left over from our visit to Cremona...

CUPCAKES ARE SO LAST YEAR. Proustian madeleines, cannellés and fashionably hued macaroons (only from Ladurée) are already tempting those that know.

HAVE YOU HEARD ABOUT THE FIRST VIENNA VEGETABLE ORCHESTRA? The entire ensemble plays on instruments made from vegetables: there's a radisynth and the hollowed courgettes with strategically placed holes are surprisingly melodic.

'*After a good dinner, one can forgive anybody, even one's own relations.*'

Oscar Wilde, playwright, poet and gastronaut.

PRODUCING A PLATTER OF CHILLI-SEARED SQUID: Did you know that capsaicin, the chemical in the chilli membrane that gives chillies their heat, is sold to completely hard-core chilli heads in wax-sealed crystal flasks? Workers at the aptly named Extreme Foods in the US have to wear sealed suits and masks to prevent them from inhaling. It is incomparably hotter that the red savina or jalapeno chilli.

MAGNANIMOUSLY HANDING ROUND THE PLATE OF SINGLE PLANTATION CHOCOLATE BARS and Paul A Young salted caramels: It really is scientifically proven that chocolate – the best sort, of course – improves one's mood. What better way to promote inner karma?

HAVE YOU HEARD PLAT DU JOUR, D.J. MATTHEW HERBERT'S DANCE MUSIC based on pots simmering, pepper grinding and the crunchy bite of an heirloom apple? The sound bites are great to prepare dinner to.

WHEN HANDING AROUND MARRONS GLACÉS (too wonderful only to have at Christmas) to special, alpha-appreciative friends, explain how true marrons glacés – delicate and almost crumbly – are laboriously repeatedly dipped in proper vanilla sugar syrup and not dunked in cornflour and sugar syrup and bruléed until tough and shiny as a shortcut. The best I've come across are from Cornucopia, even better than those I tasted in Turin.

HAVE SOME CLOTTED CREAM WITH YOUR DAMSON TART. Did you know it was originally a way of preserving the cream? It's made by gently heating the cream in a bain-marie until a honeycomb crust forms. It's best made with unpasteurised milk with high butterfat content. You must try clotted cream butter, too. It's a little crumbly and, as you can imagine, divine, but difficult to find beyond the West Country (Cornwall and Devon).

The Better Foodie movie guide to the ultimate TV-dinner
carefully pre-meditated edible and visual sustenance

Alhough we like to have a view on the latest TV-chef programmes, we're more than slightly disapproving, as frankly we'd far rather cook than watch. We prefer indulging in some of the best Foodie moments in film – those that metaphorically convey the most explosive and sensual of passions and spiritual epiphanies, making us want to step through the screen and join in with the feasting. We've collected a library of gastro-movie classics, which we're rather partial to matching with suitably evocative Foodie TV-dinners.

BABETTE'S FEAST

The ultimate Foodie film: Gabriel Axel's unsurpassed gastro-flick about Babette, a gourmet chef escapee who's cooked for decades for a couple of ascetic Danish religious sisters. Winning the lottery, she splurges it on a banquet for her employers and their puritan community. It's pure homage to the incomparable pleasure of preparing an awesome feast of exceptional ingredients, with exquisite attention to detail, for appreciative guests.

Though the Better Foodie might aspire to Blinis Davidoff (with Beluga caviar), they would probably settle for a fashionable roe – tobiko or Avruga – or substitute Blinis Romanoff with wild smoked salmon. The most haute Foodie is tempted to undertake quails en sarcophage (in pastry cases) with foie gras and truffles and chaud-froid sauce to prove they can, but for a definitve TV-supper: five-spice quail or pasta with shavings of truffle. Finish with rum baba or a pannetone alternative to kuglehopf, or simply some fresh figs.

DIM SUM

This is a poignant story following a Chinese-American family as they face the trauma of their mother dying. It focuses on the daughter's regret of not acquiring her recipes and culinary skills.

Full-on dim sum is quite a feat to prepare, even for the dedicated Foodie, but we're game to try and emulate Hakkasan's venison puffs, hoisin-glazed chai siu and prawn wontons with a chilli dipping sauce.

MY DINNER WITH ANDRE

Savour the delicious banter of Louis Malle's talkiest movie about two New York intellectuals getting together over dinner and having a confessional chat about how their lives have gone a little off-piste.

Tuck into tiny Meaux Pommery mustard lamb chops, all the more enjoyable in the privacy of your own home as they have a hands-on, juice trickling down your chin satisfaction – Better Foodies consider almost everything to taste better when eaten with their fingers.

THE GODFATHER

Not perhaps best known for its Foodiness. Devotees of the film, however, will know the scene when Clemenza teaches Michael Corleone to make marinara sauce. Chuckle approvingly as Clemenza utters the immortal line: 'Leave the gun; take the cannoli', when advising Michael what to do after he argues with crooked police captain McCluskey at a restaurant in the Bronx.

It's got to be dinner with a Sicilian slant: pasta con sarde: fresh sardines, saffron, wild fennel, currants and pinenuts, followed by Sicilian cannoli.

CHOCOLAT

Joanne Harris' exquisitely evocative ode to the charms of La France Profonde and the power of chocolate. This makes even better viewing for fortunate Better Foodies (like myself) who've had the chance to follow in Joanne Harris' footsteps and picnic by the River Baise; visit chocolatier, M Sarrouste, at La Cigale in Nerac, who inspired much of the plot; and the bastide village of Vianne, on which Chocolat was based.

Graze on a chocolate imbued tapenade (a favourite of chocolatier Chantal Coady of London's Rococco) followed by wild duck with a mole sauce and a wonderfully intense chocolate tart. Or merely sip a soothing cup of pure chocolate-flake hot chocolate and dip into a box of chocolate-enrobed Agen prunes and walnuts.

LA GRANDE BOUFFE

By turns comic, sad and bizarre: four successful middle-aged men and a woman retire to a friend's villa to enjoy a weekend of over-eating. It emerges that they plan to make it their last supper and literally eat themselves to death.

Better Foodies, naturally, have no intention of pursuing a similar fate and limit themselves to a modest salad, followed by a gargantuan helping of tarte tatin with lashings of Isigny crème fraîche.

Further Foodie film finger food

Homemade popcorn Truffled or chilli-buttered

Crispy salt and pepper tentacle-on squid
Especially good for nail-biting thrillers

Fluffy homemade taramasalata
With hot polenta-coated zucchini to dip

Posh fusion nachos With crab, melted fontina
and homemade chilli and charred tomato salsa

Madagascan vanilla ice cream Sandwiched
between homemade finest chocolate-chip cookies

Or more decadently still:
Oven roast fat chips with caviar dip; Bloody Mary
sorbet in parmesan cornets; sweet cinnamon brioche
doughnuts with warm damson jam

THE COOK, THE THIEF, HIS WIFE AND HER LOVER

Not a movie for the faint-hearted. This was considered highly controversial when it was first released, on account of Peter Greenaway's elaborately explicit displays of the sensual pleasures of eating in the fantastically bizarre Le Hollandais restaurant.

In this scenario, revenge is certainly not a dish best served cold. Dinner has to be carnivorous: 21-day-aged Buccleaugh rib eye steak with oven roasted kumera (sweet potato) chips and a bitter mâche salad.

BIG NIGHT

Enough to put even the most tempted Foodie off any flirtations with opening their own restaurant. The film follows two Italian immigrant brothers trying to save their failing restaurant in New Jersey; the conflict between High Foodie purism and catering for the masses; and the wider importance of good food bringing like-minded people together. The brothers' 'last supper' showpiece, which they called 'a bomba', is really a timballo (a grand dish which dates back to the ornate Medici family banquets when a rich assemblage of chicken liver, ham and truffles was baked together in a crisp casing of macaroni and pastry).

Settle for a more modest moulded dome of rich creamy parma ham, parmigiano reggiano, peas and carnaroli rice, or maybe the brothers' morning-after comfort food: a perfectly prepared omelette.

JAMON, JAMON

Also known as a tale of ham and passion for its examination of the lengths some will go to fulfil their lustful desire. This is a surreal and very unusual love triangle.

Best enjoyed with plenty of freshly made tortilla and a lascivious helping of Spanish jamon – preferably pata negra.

EAT DRINK MAN WOMAN

Impossible to watch without chopsticks in hand as the sensual colours and textures of the food are mesmerising. Master Taiwanese chef, Tao Chu, uses the preparation of food as a metaphor for the familial devotion he is unable to verbalise. He prepares elaborate banquets for his three daughters, who barely nibble his dishes, clearly dissatisfied with their own lives.

Hunger-inducing in the extreme, this is best watched with homemade sesame prawn toasts; five-spice soft-shelled crab; star anise, cinnamon and ginger braised brisket and steamed bok choy.

TOM JONES

A classic movie made on the threshold of the swinging 60s and based on Henry Fielding's novel, adapted by John Osborne and directed by Tony Richardson. Tom Jones (aka Albert Finney) is the 'angry young man' cynically exposing the hypocrisy of the mid-eighteenth century British aristocracy, whilst indulging his insatiable appetite for romantic adventure.

The scenes of lascivious langoustine-eating antics mean luscious crustacean dipped in something hot and buttery is de rigeur.

LIKE WATER FOR CHOCOLATE

A chocolatey family saga feast for the senses, by Laura Esquivel. Pedro and Tito are prevented from marrying as Tito's mother wants to marry off her elder daughter first and for Tito to look after her. The film uses magical realism to invite viewers to suspend belief and accept that food can affect people just by the method in which it is prepared.

The only dish to serve is baked quails with honey and rose petals, followed by a decadent chocolate guanaja fondue.

What flower does saffron come from?

It is the stamens of a saffron crocus.

What is miso?

Fermented soya bean sauce. It is mixed with dashi (a Japanese stock made from bonito flakes and kombu seaweed) to make miso soup.

What is tomalley?

The pale green liver of a lobster or crab, which retains its colour once cooked. It is a true Better Foodie delicacy to embrace.

What is beurre blanc?

A white wine, vinegar and shallot reduction, into which cubes of cold butter are whisked until the sauce is thick and smooth – perfect with roast halibut.

What is the main ingredient of piri-piri sauce?

Dried chilli peppers.

What is pain d'épices better known as?
Spicy gingerbread cake.

What is the most popular cheese requested on misson menus at NASA?
Parmigiano Reggiano – calcium craving is a result of missions in zero-gravity environments!

What does deglazing mean?
Adding stock, alcohol or water to a pan in which meat or poultry has been cooked and stirring furiously to remove the caramelised cooking juices from the base of the pan.

What is cracked pepper?
Peppercorns that have been gently whacked to crack with a mortar and pestle.

What plant family does vanilla come from?
Orchid.

CULINARY fashionability

What's moving up?
why rocket doesn't wash any longer

There's nothing like the scent of a highly directional, recondite ingredient, technique or dish to quicken the pulse of voracious Better Foodies fulsomely dedicated to expanding their personal culinary boundaries. We can't help it; we're tireless in our quest for exciting new taste experiences. We admit that it brings out the worst kind of competitive gastro-urge; we want to be the first to savour the latest tantalising trophy and serve it nonchalantly to suitably Foodie friends. But it doesn't mean that we don't care about deeper issues, too; rigorous seasonality, animal husbandry of the highest order and reduction of food miles are Foodie mantras that matter beyond fashion.

Adria-ism The inevitable question at any gregarious get-together of proper Foodies is: 'Have you eaten Adria's food at El Bulli?' It's the apogee of provocative, post-modern de-constructionist cuisine where form seems to matter as much as flavour. Whilst we're wondering whether the foams and froths are necessarily the apotheosis of haute cuisine, he's already moved on to skins, dusts and powders.

Belly pork Whilst fashion catwalk-watchers note the latest couture cut, among proper Foodies cuts of meat are a significant gastro-barometer. We simply can't get enough of rare breed pork belly or porchetta. Suckling pig and pork scratchings with provenance are back with a vengeance, too.

Rib of beef Must be hung and aged a full 28 days and have an immaculate pedigree – grass-fed Aberdeen Angus (Black Angus in the US) or, better still, Buccleuch from the Scottish borders are names to vaunt.

Pampered wagyu beef The very definition of gastronomic decadence. The densely marbled silky texture and melting tenderness is simply incomparable. The high Foodie cattle (now reared in both the US and UK, as well as in Japan) really are groomed and massaged in spa-like conditions to keep their joints supple and fed a malted beverage made from hops.

Veal Welfare-friendly reared British rose veal is perfectly acceptable to the well-informed Better Foodie who favours chops and shin of veal – the classic cut for osso buco. (Beware pale crate-confined examples.)

Brisket Canny chefs and Better Foodies look to neglected, cheaper cuts. Brisket (a lower forequarter cut of beef) is resoundingly back and is the epitome of fashionable slow-cooking for braises, roasts and barbecues.

Shoots

Call us Foodie cradle snatchers if you must.
Better Foodies are so over tasteless baby veg.,
although we adore shoots or micro-greens: hand-
harvested when they're merely centimetres high, barely
leafy and at their most tender, yet still exploding with
flavour. The committed Foodie is already growing and
snipping their own from pea and fennel to broccoli,
broad bean, French radish and red chard.

Bone marrow Beloved among fans of 'Nose to Tail' Fergus Henderson, bone marrow is the smartest accompaniment to chops, rib-eye, and even added to soups and sauces. (Better Foodies, though, will remember Nico Ladenis served bone marrow with his fabled osso buco years ago.)

Mutton No longer non-ewe (must be more than two years-old; less than this and it's called hogget) and served to a most approving royal Better Foodie, Prince Charles, at The Ritz. Mutton has a deeper, grainier texture, a more robust flavour and darker, ruby meat than younger lamb. And it ticks all the right slow-cooking Better Foodie boxes, too.

Charcuterie Always a talking point among Better Foodies who already know that pata negra (Iberican black, acorn-fed) ham with its incomparable silky nuttiness is definitely worth its high price tag. Lesser-known Le Noir de Bigorre from the Pyrenees – similarly acorn and chestnut fed – is a more affordable indulgence. Spanish cecina (air-cured, lightly smoked beef with a rich complex flavour) served simply drizzled with top-flight olive oil has eclipsed bresaola. Better Foodies are going into porcine ecstasies over culatello (literally translating as 'little arse', High Foodie Antonio Carluccio delicately tells me). This is a pear-shaped piece from the heart of the ham, brined, air-cured and considered the height of ham decadence. Sauris is an ultra-delicate version of San Daniele ham from Friuli Venezia-Giulia (the Italian Foodie region to watch, now that we know all about Puglia) and is *the* recherché charcuterie.

Cheeks are chic Both carnivorous (pork and beef cheeks, slow-cooked to caramel unctuousness) and fish cheeks (monk, halibut, grouper and hake) are no longer a well-kept secret of Basque Foodies, who've long venerated the hake and its almost meaty, yielding cheeks.

Offal Almost all Better Foodies are offalphiles to some degree and embrace ox heart, sweetbreads and pig's trotters, and veritably swoon over oxtail on restaurant menus – even if they're not quite certain about cooking such morsels at home. The hard-core Better Foodie, however, is already doing a Sunday slow-roast of pig's head, featuring cheeks and tongue. Advanced Foodies are waxing lyrical about seared monkfish liver, too – more ethical and affordable than foie gras.

Surf 'n' Turf Foodie de luxe versions of this combination are back. Dishes such as John Dory with confit belly pork, or lobster and sweetbreads, extricate the Better Foodie from agonising menu dilemmas of meat or fish.

Roe Now that the fishing of endangered wild Caspian sturgeon has been banned (even the most profligate committed Foodie can't always justify splurging on farmed caviar d'Aquitaine), the Better Foodie is turning to tobiko, or flying fish roe, sea urchin or Scandi-roes (especially bleak, perch and zander). The Better Foodie always keeps a jar of Avruga (pearlescent Spanish herring roe with a mild smoky flavour) or equally credible Onuga on stand-by, and is longing to taste salmuga and troutuga, too.

Lardo di Colonnata As Better Foodie signed-up Slow Food members know this is an extreme delicacy – the pinnacle of pork, far removed from British connotations of lard. It's made in the marble hills near Carrara in Tuscany by layering slabs of back fat from specially fattened pigs, treated with salt, herbs and spices, brined and slow-aged for a year in marble vessels. Dense and creamy, it makes a delectable Sunday evening treat on hot toast.

Tofu Rescued from health store oblivion, tofu must be freshly made and preferably served spice encrusted and gloriously blowsy within.

Wild herbs In homage to Marc Veyrat and his UK acolyte, Simon
Rogan of L'Enclume in Cumbria, wild herbs – and the more arcane the
better – are the new seasoning, especially if picked oneself. Beyond wild
garlic, look out for oxalis (or wood sorrel), sweet bracken, sweet ciceley,
chickweed, Jack-by-the-hedge and sweet woodruff.

Cress One of the few acceptably good taste garnishes to earn the
approbation of the Better Foodie, but it must be an Asian cress – preferably
nutty, peppery shiso (also known as perilla) – a piquant Greek cress with
horseradish kick or the latest cinnamon basil cress.

Mibuna and mizuna Fashionable Japanese brassicas originally from
Kyoto, all Better Foodies ensure they feature in their mesclun mix. Mibuna,
the more pungent sibling, has eclipsed rocket as the de rigeur leaf. Mizuna,
or Japanese greens, can be steamed, too.

Puntarelle The latest unfamiliar ingredient first spotted on a menu
guarantees a Better Foodie whisper frenzy and quickly filters through to our
shopping baskets. Puntarelle, which Foodies who visit Rome will already be
familiar with, is deeply directional – especially when served poltiglia (with
best extra-virgin olive oil, lemon, capers, anchovies and breadcrumbs).
The ritual of its preparation adds to its appeal: its outer leaves need to be
stripped, the core thinly sliced and put in iced water for a few minutes so
that the slices curl up – arriciatura for those Better Foodies in the know.

Scorzonera This is the kind of conversation-halting vegetable Better
Foodies thrive on. It's certainly dramatic with long, cigar-like roots and
black skin, yet tastes mildly of parsnip and makes a diverting addition to
mash or dauphinoise.

Freekah and quinoa Grains are a crucial gastro-barometer, too – remember all-pervasive polenta? A current 'in' grain among discerning Foodies is freekah: a distinctively smoked young green wheat or barley from the Middle East. Pearly, crunchy, grassy quinoa (Better Foodies know it is pro-nounced 'keenwah') is also a must. This protein-rich superfood originally grown by the Incas is actually a herb seed. It comes in ivory white, pale gold, black and even pink varieties and is much used by trail-blazing Nuevo Latino chef Douglas Rodriguez. Fregola (Sardinian couscous made from semolina) is a smart choice, too.

Smoked foods Of course, Better Foodies like the occasional treat of wild smoked salmon (preferably Forman's London-cure with its lean yet rich and delicate, slightly gamey flavour). They enjoy the frisson of exploring little-charted waters for more recherché smoked species, too, including arctic char, barracuda, snapper, Sri Lankan moda and, newest of all, smoked carp.

Lotus root crisps The Better Foodie is otherwise so over root vegetable crisps, whatever their provenance.

Green tea Not only to be drunk, this is also highly directional as a flavour (as in Salt-baked Salmon in Smoked Green Tea Bisque). All proper Foodies know green tea is crucial to Heston Blumenthal's best-loved palate cleanser: Lime-infused Green Tea Whipped with Liquid Nitrogen, Sugar Syrup and Egg White in a Double-layer Thermal Duraflask (not yet available for the Better Foodie culinary kit) and transformed into an iced meringue!

Labneh Thick strained yoghurt cheese, preferably with plenty of fresh/wild herbs and served on flatbread. Moro's Organic Chicken Stuffed with Sage and Labneh makes a stellar Foodie Sunday lunch.

Cheese

Nothing dates a faltering Foodie more ripely than cheeses beyond the cutting edge.

Burrata From Puglia, this is the luxury trade up from buffalo mozzarella. It is a stretchy, silky mozzarella filled with cream and curds; impeccably soft, buttery and fresh tasting. It must be eaten within 48 hours of making and is air-freighted to the very best delis.

Idiazabal A well-matured unpasteurised ewe's cheese from Basque Spain with defined piquant aroma and flavour; it is the next pecorino.

Raw milk British cheeses Familiarity with the latest artisan examples is taken for read.

Obscure handcrafted Spanish cheeses
Especially those with a story to tell. Impress with pungent, herbal, bitter-sweet Torta de Barros from raw Merino ewes' milk – handmade with a thistle flower rennet and spoonable, like a vacherin.

'*The discovery of a new dish does more for human happiness than the discovery of a new star.*'

Anthelme Brillat-Savarin, French lawyer, politician and writer on gastronomy, with a prodigious appetite.

Verjuice The tart juice of unripe grapes has long been championed by Australian Foodie and Barossa Valley chef, Maggie Beer. Yet it remains elusively erudite and hence appeals to Better Foodies who obsess about condiments. Verjuice mayo is sublime with poached Scottish lobster or wild seabass ceviche, and aged verjuice custard with winter rhubarb epitomises the Foodie-conscious dessert. They also like vincotto (boiled and reduced grape must, aged in oak barrels for four years) and the latest ice wine vinegar (late harvested and blended in a sherry-like Solera system).

Pastilla If it has to be pie, it must be pastilla-influenced. Authentically a feast-day Moroccan delicacy of pigeon wrapped in North African 'warqa' pastry. Fiendishly difficult to make: the spongy dough is slapped against a hot convex metal pan called a tubsil, set over hot charcoal, in a series of overlapping concentric circles to form leaves of pastry. Doyenne of Moroccan cuisine Paula Wolfert gives a full recipe; otherwise substitute filo. Pastilla is customarily highly spiced with ginger, coriander, parsley, cinnamon, saffron and harissa.

Fougasse and artisan, preferably homemade grissini, and flatbreads, such as lavash (soft and thin and often sprinkled with sesame or poppy seeds) feature in the Better Foodie bread basket, joining the already much beloved Foodie favourite: sourdough.

Create a chessert For a different take on the cheese course, emulate Patricia Michelson of London's iconic La Fromagerie by making a cheese/dessert. Use fresh unpasteurised goat's milk curd, from Charente Poitou, mixed with fresh goat's double cream blended with verjuice, acacia honey, lexia raisins, almonds, herbs and sea salt – more than likely to delight even the most cynical Foodie palate.

What's next for the avant-garde Better Foodie?

serving the next cime di rapa first

Instinctively, the committed Foodie yearns to be in the vanguard of the latest culinary trends only just stirring in the highest echelons of cheffy circles, whether they are ingredients that are ripe for a comeback (dripping – preferably goose – heated with rosemary and sea salt, or rice pudding – if the surprise success of a New York restaurant solely serving radical retakes on rice pudding is any indicator) or startlingly esoteric and thrillingly new.

BETTER FOODIES ARE EAGER TO TRY PUNGENT MUSTARD LEAF, tah tsai, red amaranth and the Japanese answer to cepes: matsutake. Plus Australian bush fruits, including quandong (with a tart apricot/peach flavour) and wild rosella (a berry/rhubarb-tasting bud); long-neglected wild berries such as whortleberry, and Scandinavian lingonberries; and more rarified Asian fruits such as dark, sweet, raisin-like slightly smoky longans – sold fresh still on their branches.

THEY'RE ALREADY FAMILIARISING THEMSELVES WITH KOREAN CUISINE, the next taste beyond Japanese. Of course, they know all about highly prized Kyoto tofu delicacies such as yoba (tofu skin) and unagi (steamed and double-charcoal-grilled eel with a sweetish caramelised crisp skin) and have done Japanese sukiyuki – a nabemono-style (one-pot) dish of ultra-tender beef, tofu, transparent konnyaku noodles (made from a taro-like starch), greens and enoki mushrooms, simmered in a shallow iron pot with shoyu, sugar and mirin – as served at cutting-edge Masa in New York. They probably make their Foodie-in-the-making-children omusubi (stuffed rice sandwiches) for their packed lunch. And they're fast acquiring a liking for kimchi (spiced, pickled and fermented cabbage), a flavour likely to transcend Korean menus, and bulgogi, the Korean version of Shabu-Shabu, barbecued at the table.

EVEN IF THE BETTER FOODIE HAS ONLY JUST RECENTLY PURCHASED AN ESPUMA, FOR CREATING FOAMS, they will be fully aware that its role may soon be eclipsed by powders and soils – from scallop and coral to chorizo – not to mention tree barks and tree essences (watch out for gellées of pine). They will have noted, too, that trailblazing chefs are serving savoury-imbued desserts with modish accents of candied olives, sage and sesame.

ALTHOUGH IT HAS LONG BEEN ACCEPTED WISDOM among Better Foodies that Italian food epitomises the paragon of simple, pristine ingredients beautifully prepared, we're pleased that crudo (raw fish and seafood flavoured with olive oils, citrus juices, herbs, spices and aromatic vegetables immediately before it is served), the Italian answer to sushi, is now gaining wider gastro-credence.

THEY'RE ALSO TALKING KNOWLEDGEABLY ABOUT SOUS-VIDE (cheffy boil-in-the-bag). This is a great technique for slow-cooking melt-in-the-mouth beef cheeks whilst infusing flavour, and Foodies would love to get their hands on the kind of state-of-the-art vac-seal and water bath kit, used at the much-talked about Midsummer House restaurant, Cambridge.

THE BETTER FOODIE IS EAGER TO TRY DISHES COOKED IN CLAY (hay or salt are so passé). The steam helps cook the – usually pescatorial – contents and the clay and bark lining adds an earthy undertone. It's all about the aroma hit when the dish is dramatically opened at table.

And what's so leftover?

The flipside is that the Better Foodie is quietly smug about not buying, cooking or ordering any former gastro-must-eats beyond their Better Foodie use-by date – unless, of course, they're consumed by an overpowering seasonal urge. Hence, beetroot has been routed out by celeriac; and kohlrabi, pinky skinned chiogga is still acceptable, as is highly seasonal sea beet. Cavolo nero has been superseded by ruby chard and there are far too many other salad leaves available – preferably Asian or heirloom – to still be excited about eating rocket. We're bored by lamb shanks and prefer the underrated and far more economical shin. We're iffy about monkfish's sustainability (although we do make an occasional concession to the cheeks) and sniffy about tuna, unless it's fatty toro belly. We're rather bored of pesto, but partial to (Marjorcan) mojo. Ciabatta is out-baked by fougasse. And, much as we adore molten-centred chocolate moelleux desserts, they're as passé as lemon tart and sticky toffee pudding; we'd far rather a medjool date and quince tatin or a dessert with a savoury edge.

Trophy extreme seasonal delicacies

how to perfect a smug supra-seasonal swagger

For Better Foodies it is not enough merely to eat in tune with the seasons and novelty is not their only trump card. Redefining gastro-notions of culinary cachet are those rare ingredients whose fleeting seasonality adds immeasurably to their allure. Inviting suitably gastrocentric friends for a spur-of the-moment just-picked hopshoot risotto on the cusp of their brief Spring season (just as those moving in elevated Venetian Foodie circles would do) epitomises the Better Foodie's devotion to the seasons.

Ormers Meaty molluscs related to abalone and akin to octopus in flavour and texture. These can only be gathered on, or up to two days after, the full or new moon in Guernsey – and only between January and April. Export is illegal, so ormer devotees must visit the island to enjoy this extreme delicacy.

Elvers Long considered a delicacy in Basque Spain (where they are better known as angulas), these transparent, matchstick-sized delicacies with a barely-there pure fishiness are best when fleetingly sautéed with garlic and chilli. They can only be fished with silk nets in the River Severn on moonlit nights during April and consequently command dizzy prices.

Hopshoots With an alluringly fleeting season between April and May. They resemble pale purple wild asparagus, though taste of almonds with a hint of artichoke and a spicy aftertaste. In Venice the brief hopshoot (or bruscandoli) season is accorded a similar fanfare to white truffles, and hopshoot risotto is treated with due reverence.

Gull's eggs Rare, tantalising and collectable only with a licence. In their brief season (May), determined Foodies can find these green/grey speckled eggs at The Ritz and Fortnum & Mason. A fishy aroma and intense eggy flavour make them an acquired taste. Small, grey pheasant eggs (with a subtle un-gamey taste similar to a pullet's egg) share an early summer season.

Samphire With a passing resemblance to wild asparagus and a moreish salty bite, early season shoots are delicious raw. Otherwise, steam them briefly and strip the flesh from the fibrous stems. It may not be food gathering at its most glamorous, but Better Foodies make a special trip to the north Norfolk coast to go ungracefully slipping and sliding knee-deep in dark, sticky mud for their trophy, only collectable June–September.

Cobnuts As all Better Foodies know this is one of the few varieties of nut native to Britain. They can only be found in Kent between late August and early October (they're only sold fresh) and are woefully under-rated. Their milky-white kernel is moist, slightly crunchy and with a hint of fresh coconut. The knowing Foodie gently roasts cobnuts drizzled with olive oil, sea salt, cracked pepper, fresh thyme and rosemary to serve with drinks, or makes the definitive Autumnal pudding: cobnut meringue, made supra-seasonal with damson compote.

Treviso or tardivo is the arch-Foodie radicchio with a transitory late Autumn season. A trophy ingredient with elongated leaves with ravishing pink striations, pronounced ribs and refreshing peppery bitterness. Eminently good with a well-aged Gorgonzola and roasted walnuts.

Vacherin A favourite Better Foodie artisan cheese. Gratifyingly gooey, washed rind cow's milk cheese with an inimitable luscious velvety texture and exuberant pungent flavour – and always sold bound in a spruce wood box. Vacherin Mont D'Or (the French version is Vacherin du Haut-Doubs) is made in the Jura on both French and Swiss sides of the border. It is only produced in small dairies during the winter months, hence its brief mid-November to February season. Baked vacherin is the only kind of fondue the Better Foodie enjoys.

Barnacles or percebes Purple-black (and frankly phallic) crustacea with a texture similar to clams. They can be found clinging to the cliffs along the Galician coast and are highly treacherous to harvest, which adds considerably to their epi-kudos – especially as they're at their briny best during the wild winter months. They can be boiled, grilled or steamed to be served with a simple buttery sauce.

Lamprey

Not actually a true fish but a primitive
vertebrate with a decidedly earthy taste, and much
relished by Finnish Foodies who feast on charcoal-
grilled lamprey between late August and October.
Lamprey bordelaise is the dish to order, during its
Spring season, in and around Bordeaux, served in
a rich red wine sauce thickened with chocolate.

Which fresh fish needs to rest for a couple of days before cooking?

Skate.

Which Italian city first introduced the rest of the world to the fork and table napkin?

Venice.

What's the difference between a New England and Manhattan chowder?

Both are soups thickened with potato and vegetables. New England's is white, without tomatoes, with salted pork belly, and is usually made with soft-shell clams; Manhattan uses hard-shell clams.

Are sweetbreads suitable for sweet-toothed vegetarians?

Certainly not. They are made from the thymus or pancreas glands of calves, lambs or pigs. Their velvety, gentle taste is considered a delicacy by carnivorous Better Foodies.

How old does cheddar have to be to be described as mature?

Nine months or more.

Which salad leaf was called 'the poor man's bread' in the nineteenth century?

Watercress.

At what age does lamb become hogget and mutton?

After a year it is hogget; on the sheep's second birthday it becomes mutton – much darker in colour, grainier and stronger in flavour.

What is ice cream served affogato?

Ice cream with hot coffee poured over it. Another instant way to razz up proper ice-cream is to drizzle with PX sherry – preferably with the addition of a few pre-macerated Málaga raisins.

What grain is used when making both Lebanese tabbouleh and kibbeh?

Bulghar or cracked wheat. Couscous is completely different, made from semolina.

What is chilli heat measured in?

Scovilles.

OUT AND ABOUT
with the
Better
Foodie

Restaurant etiquette
the Better Foodie adores eating out

We experience a frisson of excitement, with senses on full alert, as we're seated and handed a menu. But it must be the right sort of restaurant, which doesn't mean we only deign to expose our highly sophisticated palates to the swishest, starred restaurants; we'd just rather cook at home than be force-fed mediocrity. Although we may appear nonchalant about our choice of restaurant, we research meticulously; we have all the guides and are more than adept at digesting between the lines. We have favoured critics who share our discerning tastes and quirks – although we maintain a healthy disrespect for hype and largely trust our own finely tuned instinct.

WE'RE PROBABLY DISTINGUISHABLE AS BETTER FOODIES to the restaurant manager and other diners. Beyond exuding a palpable air of expectancy – without any small talk – we get down to the serious business of cross-examining the menu. Each dish is minutely discussed with irrepressible glee and we're unable to refrain from a discreet whoop when we identify a rare ingredient or a favourite producer (we're most approving of producer and regional name checks). Inevitably a pair of Foodies will hone in on the same dishes: perhaps the puntarelle salad followed by grilled Paine Farm squab with spiced pears, celery root blinis and garden lettuces. Intense negotiation will follow as to who is owed first choice.

WE'RE ALSO SAVVY ABOUT HOW MENUS WORK – we're aware that in less scrupulous establishments handwritten specials are one of the oldest ruses in the book to move slow selling dishes. Although tasting menus appeal to our adventurous spirit, we're slightly iffy about what's fundamentally the equivalent of ordering the Chinese set menu, and don't always want our palates to have to perform too many somersaults. We know our tastes and the chef's strengths and often would really rather savour more fully a couple of formidable and complementary dishes, or even confidently order our favourites off-menu.

FOODIES ARE NOT AVERSE TO EATING OUT IN LARGER PARTIES – preferably if all share similar gastro-sensibilities and play the game with questing forks to sample each and every dish.

WHAT WE REALLY ENJOY ARE DISHES THAT READ WELL AND EAT EVEN BETTER – managing that high-wire balancing act of layered (but not overly intricate) flavour, texture and technique that have you in will-it-or-won't-it-work paroxysms until the last morsel.

DISCRIMINATING BETTER FOODIES USUALLY SHY AWAY FROM 'SAFE' DISHES unless they recognise that it is the best place in the country for salt-marsh lamb or the first of the season Formby asparagus.

BETTER FOODIES POSITIVELY PURR if they are recognised as such with a special gesture – perhaps a tiny extra, unordered course or, in rare circumstances, an invitation into the hallowed kitchen.

THE BETTER FOODIE ALWAYS HAS BREAD AND CAN'T RESIST A RECHERCHÉ ROLL of adventurous flavour: saffron, seaweed or Moroccan Ras-el-Hanout, and archly approves of Echire butter – immediately recognisable by its foil and label.

THE BETTER FOODIE WILL PROBABLY ASK TO KEEP THE MENU. They think of memorizing menus as push-ups for the brain – and they really don't mind if it means the restaurant suspects that they are a deeply respected, heavily disguised critic and treats them accordingly.

Better Foodies don't allow language to be a barrier

The most self-respecting Foodies – even if they're not natural linguists – pride themselves on acquiring a good culinary grasp of French, Spanish and Italian at the very least. However, it's not rude in Foodie circles to point if you fancy something that looks good on another table but that is not immediately identifiable on the menu. Nor is it considered grandiloquently greedy to order an extra starter or main dish to have in the middle of the table so as to satisfy extreme culinary inquisitiveness.

Better Foodie essential dining out vocabulary
tip-of-the-tongue terms to better work the menu

It's akin to acquiring a linguistic batterie de cuisine and ensures the Better Foodie appears cannily cosmopolitan. The importance of knowingly appraising the menu equipped with the right vocabulary to make the crucial crunch decision of what to order can never be under-estimated. The menuese-literate Better Foodie rather enjoys scoffing at pretentious chef solecisms and tutting at the almost inevitable mis-spelt menu clangers, which occur with perplexing regularity. If still in dish-doubt, do ask.

- Agnolotti
- Baekenofe
- Cannelé
- Ceviche
- Ebi Kani
- Espetada

p15

- Fiduas
- Kimchi
- Moulard
- Orzotto
- Picado
- Tataki

p16

Abalone A greatly prized mollusc in Asian cooking, it is actually a large marine snail and only the foot is edible. Can be termed a gastropod as it comprises only one shell and one muscle.

Agnolotti Pasta squares stuffed with veal, breadcrumbs and plenty of parmesan cheese, dressed with the meat juices or butter, Piedmontese style.

Baekenofe Alsacienne dish of long marinated pork loin, lamb and brisket, baked with potatoes, onion, leeks, carrot and Riesling. Oxtail and pig's trotter are often added. Danny Meyer, of MOMA's highly acclaimed new restaurant, The Modern, has a new take on this dish using tripe and conch as well as the usual pork.

Barba di frate A wild vegetable that looks like a long straggling, thick bunch of chives and tastes rather like samphire or young spinach – best with olive oil and lemon or garlic.

Beurre noisette Literally translates as 'nut butter'. It is achieved by caramelising the milk/protein element of butter. Take it a little further and burn the sediment for black butter – a classic skate accompaniment.

Caesar salad Made with cos lettuce, garlic, olive oil, croutons, parmesan and Worcestershire sauce (pounded anchovies should only feature in the dressing and chicken is considered an abomination).

Cannelé Traditionally made in Bordeaux. A milky, eggy batter is infused with rum and baked in special moulds. Notoriously difficult to make perfectly – Pierre Hermé in Paris and bakery/restaurant Le Comptoir Gascon in London serve the best examples.

Carta di musica or pane carasa Sardinian unleavened, crackly-thin bread…utterly addictive.

Ceviche Fish that has been marinated, or 'cooked', in citrus juices.

Compôte Fruit cooked in syrup, often with spices.

Confit A term traditionally used to signify meats that have been salted and cooked slowly in their own fat and preserved. Strictly-speaking it refers to duck (moulard) confit, synonymous with southwest France. Confit duck is used in cassoulet and garbure (a fragrant duck fat, vegetable and tarbais bean soup). Confit is, however, often misused indiscriminately to denote ingredients cooked down slowly.

Crepe parmentier A fluffy, buttery potato omelette. 'Parmentier' simply means topped with mashed potato.

Crépinette A small sausage with herbs – and sometimes truffles – wrapped in caul. It is then grilled, sautéed or baked. May be used to stuff guinea fowl or fried and served with oysters.

Ebi kani Soft, rice-paper spring roll stuffed with a mixture of crunchy shrimp, salad and spicy Japanese mayo.

Espetada A Madeiran dish of beef or lamb marinated for several days in red wine, oil, garlic, bay leaf and peppercorn, then grilled on a skewer.

Fiduas Braised short noodles from Catalonia, usually served as an accompaniment to a seafood stew – as a form of paella.

Carpaccio

Strictly speaking this is used to mean 'thin slices of raw beef'. Its name derives from the Renaissance painter, Carpaccio, who used beef-red colour extensively in his work. Unforgiveables such as pineapple carpaccio are the very worst kind of menuese abuse.

Five-spice powder A traditional Chinese mix of cinnamon, cloves, fennel seeds, Sichuan peppercorns and star anise.

Gravadlax Salmon cured in salt and sugar for several days. Curing encourages the cells and tissues of the fish to break up, resulting in a softness similar to cooked or cured fish, whilst retaining the fresh zing of raw fish.

Head cheese Not a cheese at all, but a sausage made from the meaty bits of the head of a calf or pig, seasoned, combined with a gelatinous meat broth and cooked in a mould. Usually served cold.

Involtini Rolled meat – usually veal or beef – with a stuffing bound with egg and parmesan and sautéed in butter and Marsala.

Kimchi Fiery hot fermented cabbage – a Korean speciality now making wasabi-like in roads onto wider menu repertoire.

Meunière Lightly floured fish, fried in butter, served with lemon juice, nut butter and parsley.

Miso Fermented paste of soy beans and usually rice or barley. White miso is sweeter with a fine texture and is much used in soups and dressings.

Moulard A breed of duck with a thick meaty breast, raised primarily for its larger fatty liver for foie gras. Its breast, often aged for a week or more, is referred to as magret.

Onglet or hanger steak Very tender, plump steak (from abdominal muscles); a cut increasingly in favour.

'An empty stomach
is not a good
political advisor.'

Albert Einstein, scientist, mathematician and humanist.

Nuggets of Foodie knowledge you ought to know

filling the gaps we'd rather not have in our epicurious education

The consummate Better Foodie does not settle for delayed gratification, rather greedily anticipates the next hot topic of gastronomic discussion and pre-reads voraciously on pertinent Foodie matters. Occasionally, however, and I've even known stellar chefs to be caught on the hoof, a crucial culinary gap comes to light – a matter which can be pre-empted by thorough digestion of this core curriculum.

Which parts of a crab can't you eat?
The dead men's fingers, which are the grey feathery looking bits behind the flip-side of the outer shell (basically the gills, and unpalatably bitter). Remove, along with the poo pipe and stomach sack. Twisting/cracking the joints and claws and picking out every last morsel of meat using a crab/lobster pick or narrow teaspoon is, however, de rigeur.

How to ask for more tea in a Chinese restaurant:
Balance the lid of the teapot on the handle or turn it upside down to request a refill. The pro taps two fingers on the table as a gesture of thanks.

Should oysters be swallowed or chewed?
Oyster aficionados always chew the oyster slowly and deliberately to get the full-on briny flavour. Immediately swallowing oysters whole is for wimps.

What exactly are rum babas?
These are made from savarin dough, sweet with plenty of yeast. They are baked in small ring-moulds and then drenched in rum-infused syrup. Currently the modish Parisian dessert.

What gives away a faux sourdough?
Sourdough should feel relatively heavy for its size. If it is too light and squidgy, it will be yeast assisted and lack the distinctive rich, sweet yet acidic flavour and keeping qualities of the genuine loaf.

Does salt-marsh lamb taste salty? And why is it so special?
It shouldn't taste salty – unless the cook has over-seasoned it! The lambs are grazed on tidal marshland where they feed on lichen, mosses, samphire et al. The meat has a distinctive, almost grainy texture and a darker colour.

Should eggs be kept in the fridge or not?

Eggs deteriorate four times faster at room temperature (according to kitchen chemistry guru Howard McGee) and the dreaded salmonella bacterium can thrive in the warmth, so keep your eggs in the fridge. Ideally take them out an hour or so before you use them, however, for better whipping, boiling etc.

How to spot the dim sum connoisseur:

The number of pleats in the har gau (steamed sweet prawn dumpling) should be more than ten – a sure sign of advanced dimsumology.

Why do roast meats need a rest before eating?

As the residual heat from the exterior of the meat works its way into the cooler centre, the roast will gently continue to cook. As the heat evens out, the juices in the meat are then redistributed more evenly. This explains why a roast that has been carved immediately will ooze twice as much juice as one that has rested, and will turn out overly dry in parts.

How do you eat globe artichokes?

Boil whole until tender and, working inwards towards the centre, dip leaf by leaf into melted butter. Then slice off the hairy choke, before eating the prized heart. Young violet artichokes have edible chokes: trim off the spiky top leaves, halve (unless they are real babes) and bake or sauté in olive oil. Finish with lemon and black pepper.

Why is it best not to stuff a bird?

Little heat reaches the central cavity of the bird until quite late in roasting, so the stuffing won't cook properly and will slow down the overall roasting time of the bird. It is much better to put any stuffing directly under the skin at the neck, which will also help protect the breast meat during cooking.

Couveture, ganache, gianduja or praline?

Couveture is high cocoa solid/cocoa fat chocolate, which melts and covers easily and is used to enrobe ganache. Beware inferior chocolatiers or melters: however deceptive their fancy packaging they merely buy in ready-made couveture.

Ganache is melted chocolate and cream and is the basis of most truffles and filled chocolates.

Gianduja is an irresistible Piedmontese combination of roasted hazlenuts and chocolate – Gobino in Turin make the best.

Praliné is a French word used to describe a chocolate made with roasted almonds and/or hazlenuts ground together with caramel. Confusingly, Belgians, such as Pierre Marcolini, call all filled chocolates pralines.

What's the difference between pancetta and streaky bacon?

Pancetta comes from the same pork belly cut, but the salt cure used is flavoured with herbs and spices such as garlic, pepper and fennel seeds. And, unlike bacon, pancetta is air-cured for four months.

What's the difference between sugar and cane sugar?

Sugar (white only) is refined from European sugar beet; cane is refined from tropical sugar cane.

When cooking pasta is there any benefit in adding olive oil?

This is completely pointless and is regarded with absolute bafflement by Italian Better Foodies. It makes the pasta slippery and less able to absorb the sauce. A quick stir as the water comes back to the boil is all that is required to prevent pasta sticking together.

Does my rice need rinsing?

Emphatically not. All Better Foodies know that rice is around 80 per cent starch and so it defeats the whole point of rice to try to diminish its starch content by rinsing it. What's more, it's impossible to make a decent risotto or pilaf with wet rice grains, which repel the fat.

How can farmers suddenly be selling so many slow-growing traditional breed sheep?

This is a contentious area. Most farmers don't have the land to support all the slow-reared produce that they'd like to sell. Scrutinising traceability may reveal that some animals are born elsewhere – hopefully living and feeding as well as on their 'adopted' farmstead, and reared organically if they are to be sold as such. To be sold as their own at farmers' markets, they must be 'finished' for at least six months on the named farm.

What makes vanilla extract different to, and far pricier than, vanilla essence?

Pure vanilla extract is made by crushing cured, fresh vanilla pods with alcohol to extract the vanillin (the compound that gives vanilla its aroma and flavour). Cheaper vanilla essence is made from a synthetic compound and is no substitute at all.

Chopsticks or no chopsticks and how to soy dip:

The Japanese always eat sushi with their fingers rather than with chopsticks and they never add wasabi to their soy. Dip fish side down into the soy, otherwise the rice collapses, and, very importantly, place the sushi fish side down on your tongue for maximum pleasure.

Is my lobster fresh?

The colour of a live lobster will vary according to its habitat but will usually be blue or greenish. It will move its legs and antennae and flip its tail. Live lobster must not be stored in fresh water, but in an insulated box with jell-ice/seaweed, or under a damp cloth in the fridge. On cooking, the lobster loses its ability to curl its tail underneath its body, and the tail itself loses its elasticity. A cooked lobster should, therefore, have a curled tail – indicating that it was alive when it was cooked. After being cooked, all lobsters are red, as the predominant red pigment in the shell is released on immersion in boiling water. The antennae of cooked lobster can easily be pulled out. The greenish tomalley (the liver) that is revealed when the tail is separated from the body is considered a great delicacy, as is the roe.

How to identify a sushi master:

The sure sign of a true sushi master is that every five grains of rice will face in the same direction!

The Foodie epicurean explorer
going gastro-places in search of Foodie paradise

It's non-negotiable: the Better Foodie invariably books a holiday around the destination's eating potential, whether a hallowed A-list hotspot such as Paris, New York or Barcelona or an emerging region of rich culinary gratification, preferably factoring in sun and lush scenery, besides suitably rare and recherché indigenous ingredients. On returning from rewarding epicurean travels, the Better Foodie will launch into a super-charged flurry of entertaining to showcase their latest gastro-discoveries.

THE BETTER FOODIE TRAVELLER IS ALWAYS WELL-PREPARED and relishes researching dishes to sample, the supra-specialist providores to stock up at (not only for ingredients, but arcane culinary implements, too; Joel Robuchon always buys the finest mesh sieves for his legendary pomme purée in the Kappabashi-don 'Kitchen Town' district of Tokyo), the hallowed markets to soak up the sights, sounds, smells and tastes of the food culture, and food-focused festivals not to be missed.

ENDEAVOUR TO TRAVEL LIGHT, allowing plenty of spare capacity in your luggage for inevitably getting carried away when purchasing irresistible comestibles and kitchen hardware. Often, an unidentifiable, pungent yet rather enticing whiff emanating from a plane's overhead locker is enough to identify the Better Foodie on a gastro-break.

Rising on the Better Foodie's gastronomic radar

fifteen of the palate-pleasing places a Better Foodie must visit

Once the high-rolling, destination-ticking faux Foodies have moved in, the Better Foodie moves on in search of fresh and extra-virgin tasty territory. Ever hungry for gastro-adventure, we rate local food above luxury and will travel great, time-consuming, appetite-whetting distances in pursuit of new, or at least reassuringly undiscovered, gastro-nirvana – whether chilli and lime conch, giant sea snail of memorable, wake-up freshness or a lesser known culinary trump gastro-location (perhaps Lyon's characterful, offalphile and pike dumpling bouchons), which have long (and quietly) held local Foodies enthralled, and challenge our culinary boundaries.

San Sebastian, Spain

According to Ferran Adria (of world-famous Spanish restaurant, El Bulli), this is probably the best place in the world in terms of the outstanding quality of food you will be served from any place you happen to walk into. Elegant San Seb has more Michelin stars per capita than anywhere else (15 at the last count) and has thriving Basque sociedad gastronomica clubs, the men-only 'brotherhoods' who get together solely to cook, eat and discuss food – favoured Foodies can occasionally infiltrate.

WHAT TO SAVOUR: Bacalao croquetas, anchovies and glistening marbled pata negra are everywhere. Also try kokotxas (the membrane from the throat of the hake, considered a great delicacy) in salsa verde; sea scorpion stew; marmitako (a traditional Basque fish stew with bonito and potato); and perfect pulpo (boiled octopus) with paprika. Recondite specialities include percebes and lampreys from the Galician coast.

WHERE TO EAT: Dazzling Pintxo (pronounced pin-cho) are the Basque take on tapas. The locals navigate them by way of the txikiteo, stopping for just one el especialidad del casa in each bar. Alona Berri, repeated winner of the annual Concurso de Pintxos contest, has artfully dramatic morsels: baby squid with an octopus and martini shot and caramelised rice; Casa Gandarias is Foodie heaven for foie gras pinxtos, lamb brochette, sizzling kidneys, seafood and tortilla; and Txepetxa is a temple for anchovies. Make a gastro-pilgrimage to the legendary father and daughter kitchen of Arzak, and rising star Andoni Luis Aduriz of Mugaritz for grilled foie in consomme, and lightly poached tuna with stems, leaves and lily petals.

WHAT TO BRING BACK: Idiazabal (a much-prized, semi-soft sheep's milk cheese with distinctive rind), pata negra ham, definitive tinned anchovies, pimientos de padron and smoked pimenton, membrillo, saffron and turron (jijona is soft and crumbly; alicante is crisp, textured with chopped nuts).

Franche-Comté, Northeast France

Close to the Swiss border, sandwiched between the Jura mountains and immense pine forests and surrounded by palpably pure air, this is fast gathering pace on the Francophile Better Foodie's barometer.

WHAT TO SAVOUR: Bliss for cheese devotees: aged Comté – redolent of brioche and hazlenut, and strictly seasonal and riotously ripe Vacherin, wrapped in fragrant spruce bark. Also, pike and char with crayfish; friture (tiny freshwater fish deep-fried); chicken with morels and vin jaune.

WHERE TO EAT: Refined menu terroir at Le Bon Accueil in Malbuisson or Chateau de Germigney in Port Lesney. Auberge de la Grangette, at 1,900 metres high in the Jura, is the ultimate place to enjoy resin-scented, rich Vacherin, baked in its box – with smoked morteau sausage, local ham and potatoes to indulgently dip.

WHAT TO BRING BACK: A Comptoise cheeseboard of aged Comté, bleu de Gex and Morbier (Vacherin doesn't travel well.) Also, bottled Griotte cherries from Fougerolles.

The Better Foodie reserves well ahead

Yet certainly doesn't believe in sticking rigidly to schedules, especially when an unexpected eating opportunity arises. Nor do Better Foodies take the restaurant guides as gospel – they're always hoping to chance upon a wondrous, as yet undiscovered, gem of a hole-in-the-wall authentic edible find, and won't be able to help themselves flaunting such trophy food experiences to their Better Foodie friends. They consider hours spent perusing menus and specialities in pursuit of choosing the right place for the next great meal as gripping as the latest thriller.

Brittany, France

Fashionable once more, especially among discerning Parisian Foodies, the smaller seaside towns ooze old-fashioned Dufy charm. Better Foodies relish still-slapping fish and sea-pert squiggling seafood straight from the boat. Towns like Pont L'Abbé and Quimper are ineffably chic, while Finistère is wilder and reminiscent of Cornwall.

WHAT TO SAVOUR: The freshest briny Belon oysters straight out of the sea – half a dozen, half a bottle of Muscadet, a properly crusty baguette and Echire butter overlooking the oyster beds make for a deeply memorable mid-afternoon snack. Deeply sybaritic for crustacea devotees: ravishing langoustines, sweet crevettes gris, etrille or velvet crab, skate cheeks and cotriade (the local fish stew). Also competing for the Better Foodie's tastebuds: purple tinged artichokes, Plougastel strawberries, salted caramel ice cream, Breton far, galettes and crépes.

WHERE TO EAT: Satisfyingly off the beaten track and low key, an unassuming coastal bar with a gloriously old school fish restaurant above, Le Doris, in the tiny port of Kerity, is stuffed to the gills with locals. It offers the best lobster – served in two helpings – that I've ever experienced. At the other extreme is Les Maisons de Bricourt in Cancale (the newest three Michelin star status restaurant in France) where tantalising local seafood is given delicate global spice treatments.

WHAT TO BRING BACK: Sel de Guérande, vintage sardines, kouign-amann – a sweet buttery folded yeast cake – and petit beurre biscuits.

Orkneys, UK

Remote, with awe-inspiring huge skies and clean seas. Challenging to reach, this adds to the allure and means much of the best produce (a combination of ancient rural foods and superlative seafood) stays on the Islands.

WHAT TO SAVOUR: North Ronaldsay lamb (a one-off, semi-feral, gamier-tasting breed fed almost entirely on seaweed); far gamier meat and outstanding game – especially grouse, woodcock, teal, and widgeon; beremeal bannocks; indigenous Creel sea witch (like lemon sole); forkbeard (similar to ling); superlative scallops, langoustines and lobster; sea lettuces; machair potatoes and rowanberries.

WHERE TO EAT: In a time warp, the gloriously old-fashioned Creel restaurant serving deliciously fresh Orkney hand-dived scallops, crab, megrim, and seaweed-fed mutton from North Ronaldsay. Cosy Hamnavoe, in the seventeenth-century harbour town Stromness, with views to Scapa Flow and fish straight off the boats: cullen skink, haddock with lobster sauce and inordinately plump coral-on scallops.

WHAT TO BRING BACK: Lobster, smoked fish, Orkney fudge, beremeal.

Better Foodies like to provide their own sustenance for the journey

A tray of sushi or a well-spiced chickpea salad for the plane (altitude affects even the Better Foodie's taste buds – the oddities of air pressure mean dishes need extra spicing); an artisan pork pie and hastily made treviso, black grape and walnut salad for a long train journey; maybe a couple of heritage apples and a bar of Valrhona Manjari for the car.

County Cork, Ireland

Ireland's Foodiest region, stuffed with artisan food producers – reflected in the distinctive 'road map' menus that name-check producers' provenance.

WHAT TO SAVOUR: Crubeens (crispy pig's trotters, cooked first in stock) and Roscarbery lobster. Irish chef Richard Corrigan is a devotee of trout and salmon from Frank Hederman's Belvelly Smokehouse at Cobh.

WHERE TO EAT: For wonderful dining and cookery courses (including wild foods and breads) visit Ballymaloe in Midleton started by Myrtle Allen (founding mother of the Irish Slow Food movement and in the vanguard of seasonally driven eating). Try Café Paradiso for excellent seasonal vegetarian food. Cork Farmgate uses products straight from the English Market, including tripe and drisheen (sheep blood sausage). Also, Longueville House, Mallow, for its virtually self-sufficient, ultra-seasonal menu.

WHAT TO BRING BACK: Gubbeen, Milleens and farmhouse Durrus cheeses, aged Imokilly cheddar – sold only at Ballymalloe; hand-roasted Macroom oatmeal; Krawczyk's Bolg Doire (a West Cork salami from dry-cured free-range pork belly) and Irish pastrami; comestibles from Midelton Market – the Irish riposte to Borough market.

Lisbon, Portugal

All the better for being the least recognised Med cuisine. Relish beautiful squares, flamboyant Art Nouveau and tile-covered façades, steep, narrow lanes in Barrio Alto and a mix of old-fashioned tascas serving grilled sardines. Time allowing venture beyond into the Alentejo region.

WHAT TO SAVOUR: Baked caldeirada de bacalhau; unctuous velvety Serra cheese scooped out with a spoon (using the thistle flower of cardoons instead of rennet); chourico (pork marinated in red wine, paprika, garlic, smoked over holm oak, then air-cured); Alentejano marbled, intensely aromatic black acorn-fed pata negra; pumpkin and walnut jam; the legendary Antiga Confeitaria de Belem, for pasteis de nata (creamy, eggy, scorched and golden, flaky custard tarts hot from the oven, sprinkled with cinnamon).

WHERE TO EAT: Flores, in the svelte Hotel Bairro Alto, for chef-of-the-moment Henrique Sa Pessoa's traditional Portuguese cuisine with an Asian edge. For Michelin-starred seafood: Porto de Santa Maria and Eleven, and for more refined seafood try Varenda at The Four Seasons.

WHAT TO BRING BACK: Buttery queijo da Serra; charcuterie from Mercado da Riberia; flower of sea salt with oregano; Alentejo single estate extra virgin olive oil; carrot and almond, and melon and walnut Sabores do Monte artisans jams and Elvas plums.

'*A good cook is like
a sorceress who
dispenses happiness.*'

Ella Schiaparelli, flamboyant 1930's fashion designer.

The Better Foodie has a number of short Foodie breaks throughout the year...

...planned to coincide with the season for a local delicacy or to attend an unmissable epicurean one-off – the week in New York when many iconic restaurants slash their prices (early February); the violet festival in Toulouse (February); the Lyth valley in the UK's northwest, when the damson blossom is in season and the last harvest's damson cheese just ready (March); the truffle fair in Alba (October); or Slow Food's Salone del Gusto, biennially in Turin (October). In essence, it's the Better Foodie, modern day equivalent of undertaking the Grand Tour – experiencing the world on a plate.

Fruili-Venezia Giulia, Northeast Italy

A satisfyingly under-discovered region stretching almost the entire way from Venice to Vienna, taking in the Alps and the Adriatic coast. It has Ottoman and Central European culinary influences.

WHAT TO SAVOUR: Unusual flavour combinations – particularly mixing fruit with savoury: polenta with cinnamon aged ricotta, and gnocchi with plums. Also try potato strudel with radicchio and wild fennel; Carso beef with horseradish; Frico croccante fritters made with Montasio (local tangy cow's milk cheese); orzotto (barley risotto) with red turnip and Carso ham; San Daniele proscuitto and Sauris hams; musseto (a sausage made from pig's snout) and strudel with dried fruit and chocolate.

WHERE TO EAT: Trattoria Gostilia Develak, at San Michele del Carso, has been in the same family since 1870 and has an Italian/Slavic slant to its menu. Also worth a visit is Vitello d'Oro in Udine. Sample the risotto with treviso and local salsiccie, salt cod in filo and Adriatic frito misto.

WHAT TO BRING BACK: Sauris, San Daniele and other charcuterie, Montasio cheese and brovoda (a cross between turnip and radish, pickled in grape juice), which even your most forward-thinking fulsome Better Foodie soulmates may not yet have tried.

Veneto, Italy

Gathering pace on the Italophile Better Foodie barometer is neighbouring Veneto. This has similarly been long overlooked as a Foodie haven.

WHAT TO SAVOUR: Classic dishes to sample include: riso e bisi (rice and fresh peas), fegato alla Veneziana (calves liver with caramelised onions), bigoli in salsa (traditional hand extruded, long flat spaghetti with a hole, with anchovy and slow-cooked onions), chiodini mushrooms from Montello, radicchio di Treviso and white asparagus from Bassano. Also try risotto bruscandoli (hopshoots) in Spring, baccala creamed with polenta, molleche (soft shell lagoon crabs), inky cuttlefish, mazzancolle (enormous Mediterranean shrimps) and other wondrous fish at il Mercato di Pesce – probably the most beautiful seafood market in the world.

WHERE TO EAT: Da Fiore is *the* iconic Venetian restaurant – its Moleche soft-shell crab and pot-roasted sea clams are legendary. Naranzaria, on the Grand Canal, is a wine bar/restaurant. In the bar, sample the chicetti (bite-size snacks) and aperitivo, and in the restaurant, the carpaccio of branzino (sea bass) and Pantelleria caper flowers; orzotto (barley risotto) with asparagus, peas and chanterelles; and polenta with cherry tomatoes and basil. Le Calandre, on Bisol's agriturismo estate, offers sophisticated gourmandising, too. Florian, Europe's first coffee house, dating back to the eighteenth century, is still much favoured.

WHAT TO BRING BACK: Radicchio di Treviso, recondite condiments, artisan bigoli pasta, biscottini (including delicate baicoli for zabaglione/coffee), Bussol (a yeasty Easter cake made only on Burano).

Sardinia, Italy

Inexplicably relatively under-discovered by epicurean travellers, it is even feasible as a European Foodie weekend break. There are stunning wild coasts with pink rock, secret swimming coves, rugged myrtle and juniper covered hills and romantic Phoenician ruins.

WHAT TO SAVOUR: Spit-roasted kid or porceddu (suckling pig) with sea salt and myrtle; malloreddus pasta; wild boar charcuterie; parchment-thin carta di musica/pane fresa (moreish Sardinian flatbread); fregola (a couscous like pasta) with sea bream sauce; bocconi cannoli (deep-fried cone-shaped pastries voluptuously filled with ricotta, candied fruits and chocolate).

WHERE TO EAT: Su Gologone for the legendary myrtle-infused spit-roast suckling pig, aubergine pie, ricotta and honey ice-cream; in medieval Alghero, Il Pavone, for fresh anchovies and marinated sardine antipasti, cuttle fish and fava bean pasta, red mullet with tomato and basil and crema catalan, betraying the town's Catalan influence; Il Faro in Oristano for superb fregodina with clams, tuna milt, pinzimonio (stunning vegetable crudités served after the main dish with olive oil to dip) and seadas (grilled pastries filled with pecorino and melassa di miele – bitter honey). Visit Taverna della Marina in the capital, Cagliari, for malloreddus (gnocchi-like saffron pasta with sea bream sauce). Near to Cagliari, next to the ruins of the ancient city of Nora, L'Appardo di Anfitrite (a restored coastal country home) serves straccetti with sea urchins and almonds and culingiones (handmade pasta parcels filled with potatoes and mint) accompanied by bottarga sauce.

WHAT TO BRING BACK: Bottarga (a dried and salted grey mullet roe), pecorino sardo from Il Formaggiaio in Cagliari or Antichi Saperi in Alghero.

'Strange to see how a good dinner and feasting reconciles everybody.'

Samuel Pepys, diarist and gourmet, who reputedly buried a Parmigiano Reggiano rather than risk it being destroyed by The Great Fire of London.

Croatia

Although no longer the Med's best-kept Foodie secret, it is still reassuringly under-discovered, despite its spectacular Adriatic coast, wild interiors and plentiful konobas (homely, family-run restaurants). Better Foodies are keen to keep such gems to themselves.

WHAT TO SAVOUR: Refreshingly different, gutsy Mediterranean food: gently salty sheep's cheese served with rosemary-infused honey; gregado (slow-cooked scorpion, fish, mussel and potato stew); honey; buzura (shellfish stew); bay and rosemary-braised chicken with gnocchi; prsut (home-cured hams); Istrian truffles; cherry and curd cheese strudel.

WHERE TO EAT: Sesame Tavern close to Dubrovnik's Old Town; Pile Gate, for orange marinated monkfish carpaccio and gregado; Zori restaurant, on the Pakleni archipelago, for clams with rosemary and capers and crispy skinned salpa fish; Restaurant Gverovic-Orsan – designer rustic and offers spectacularly good charcoal-grilled fish on a private beach close to Dubrovnik; Kanoba Jastozera, a Lobster House on wooden stilts over Komiza's bay on Vis Island, which specialises in charcoal-grilled and brodet lobster (in herby tomato stew). For sublime truffles: Istria's Zigante Tartufi.

WHAT TO BRING BACK: Istrian low-acidity olive oil with a peppery kick; herb infused honey; young goat's cheese with rosemary; capers and truffles.

Melbourne, Australia

Australia's most upwardly epicurious city and completely obsessed by food. **WHAT TO SAVOUR:** Queen Victoria market is the largest in the Southern hemisphere and has more than 1000 traders (including Holy Goat and Tarago River artisan cheeses). Also pay a visit to the summer night-time hawker's market. Join a Tony Tan culinary tour/cooking class for a Malaysia-meets-Australian-ingredients eye-opening experience or a Campion and Curtis tour (authors of Melbourne's annual Foodie guide). **WHERE TO EAT:** Richmond Hill Café and Larder, formerly owned by iconic cookery writer/cook Stephanie Alexander and still a gastro haven (with a good cheese room); Greg Malouf's much lauded MoMo for exotic Levantine cuisine; Donovan's, a 1920s beachside bathing-house-turned-restaurant, for zingy barbequed fish; Providore for a Better Foodie brunch. Visit Taxi, in futuristic Federation Square, for adventurous dining with Japanese leanings: roast rabbit saddle, shiitake mushrooms, yabbie tails and sweet-sour dressing; or the Ping Eatery and Bar in Port Melbourne, for beachside contemporary Vietnamese/dim sum. The Foodie press is currently swooning over Thai-influenced Longrain, newly arrived in Melbourne, and the ultra-sophisticated Cantonese delicacies of The Flower Drum. **WHAT TO BRING BACK:** Chocolates from Haigh's, obscure Australian delicacies from Alimentari, Asian delicacies from Queen Victoria market.

Damascus, Syria

This is the oldest continuously inhabited city in the world – where feasting is a national preoccupation! The Old City is a vibrant labyrinth of mosques, minarets, souks and traditional Arab frescoed houses restored as restaurants.

WHAT TO SAVOUR: Abundant mezze include baba ganoush with aubergine and sesame, bakdounis (parsley and tahini) and labneh makbus (yoghurt cheese balls); za'tar rubbed khoubz (a flatbread baked on a large metal dome called a sorj); salads: fattoush (tomatoes and cucumber with flatbread and sumac) and parsley and burghal (cracked wheat) tabouleh. Sample: Fataih (ground lamb mixed with browned almonds and parsley), sfiha (flat lamb pies with cinnamon, pine nuts and pomegranate molasses) and kibbeh (finely ground and kneaded lamb with burghul, all-spice, and often pinenuts) – the measure of excellence among Arabic cooks. And try Kibbeh Nayye, the Syrian take on steak tartare. Street food cooked-to-order includes falafel and chicken schwarma with garlic mayo and sour pickles.

WHERE TO EAT: Former homes of Damascene aristocracy turned into sumptuous restaurants with courtyard gardens, complete with fountains, orange trees and marble mosaics – Zeituna and Barjiz are addresses to relish. Al Halabi, within The Four Seasons hotel, serves definitive refined classics including kibbeh with quince and pomegrante.

WHAT TO BRING BACK: Za'tar; almond and pistachio Arabic sweets soaked in orange flower or rose syrup, and date crescents from Semiramis stores; a long-handled rakwi coffee pot, tahrini brass coffee grinder, cardamom infused coffee and cinnamon walnut tea from Souk Hamidiyeh.

Salvador De Bahia, Brazil

In the north-eastern corner of Brazil, and gastronomically under rated –
except by savvy Brazilian Better Foodies – vibrant Pelourinha (the historic
district) is a maze of winding cobbled streets of pastel colonial buildings
(many of which are converted into restaurants), superb beaches, with music
everywhere and a strong African influence. Better Foodies time their visit to
dovetail with the Bahia Carnavale in February.

WHAT TO SAVOUR: Claypot-cooked, crab-rich seafood moqueca with
spicy tomato sauce enjoyed with cornbread; churrasco (spit-roast beef) and
chimichurri (parsley, garlic and vinegar sauce) with farofa (tapioca pancakes);
acarajè (deep-fried bread of mashed black-eyed beans) stuffed with camarao
(sun-dried shrimp), hot-pepper sauce and vatapà (a special paste of shrimps,
peanuts, cashews and coconut milk) sold by Baianas de Acaraje (street sellers
dressed in white) who also offer quejo fundido (charcoal-grilled salt cheese
with oregano). From the baracas (bars around Mercado Modelo) snack on
cups of lambretas caldo (local mussels steamed in a herb broth); aguilinhas
(freshly fried anchovies) and moela (spicy chicken gizzards). For dessert:
Portuguese-influenced quindim (coconut and egg upside-down cake); exotic
fruits; coffee purchased from cafezinho (ambulant coffee salesmen).

WHERE TO EAT: Restaurant Yemanjá, overlooking the bay, for sun-dried
meats served with orange, kale, cassava, and hot pepper and lemon sauce,
lobster, crab or shrimp camarao stews, and feijoada (spicy stewed black eye
beans); Mama Bahia for the best bolinhos (deep-fried rice and cheese balls).

WHAT TO BRING BACK: Ceramics from Mercado Modelo, hot pepper
sauce and hot chilli peppers, Brazilian black beans, tinned palm hearts,
rocambole cakes filled with guava paste, beijinho de coco, coconut fudge,
coffee, Yerba mate (a herbal beverage with hints of green tea, coffee or
tobacco) and traditional gourd drinking vessel and bombilla (a special metal
straw/sieve for sipping what is reputedly a rejuvenating drink).

Georgia, Asia

Temptingly exotic yet still relatively unchartered for Foodie visits. Georgian lavish hospitality is justly legendary as are their ritualised supra feasts, undertaken simply when welcoming a guest. Listening to the tamada, or toastmaker (who gives traditional toasts to friendship, the country et al) is essential to understand the intricacies of how and when to commence what inevitably turns out to be a veritable banquet.

WHAT TO SAVOUR: Start a meal with badrijani bazhashi (walnut-stuffed aubergine), lobio (green bean, coriander and walnut salad) or basturma (air-dried pastrimi-like cured beef). Follow with satsivi chicken with walnut, garlic, cinnamon and fenugreek sauce; pungent spiced shashlik grilled meats served with chilli pepper sauce; or chanakhi (aubergine, tomato, basil and mutton stew) and khachapuri (a wonderful folded yeast bread bulging with salty white, stringy cheese). Whole cafés are devoted to khinbali – steamed giant dumplings with spiced meat and sauce, traditionally eaten, messily, with fingers, using the pleated dough 'lid' to pick up the hot dumplings.

WHERE TO EAT: In the capital Tbilisi, Mukhrantubani is a nineteenth-century building full of Georgian culinary artefacts. It is situated next to the sulphur baths and is renowned for its menu of khinkali – Better Foodies approve of the pour-your-own homemade pomegranate molasses to accompany the grilled fish. The velvet-walled Khinkali House serves wild mushrooms alongside meat khinkali and sturgeon shashlik. The Golden Fleece specialises in Western Georgian cuisine including mzwadi (grilled chicken, pork or beef with onions, pomegranate kernels and sour sauce). The Bread House is well known for its Adjarouli khachapuri, with a quivering soft egg and butter on the top.

WHAT TO BRING BACK: Adjika (a paste of crushed walnuts, garlic and spices), Chuchkhela (stringed walnuts dipped in thickened grape juice syrup and dried as candied walnuts), tubs of caviar; hazlenuts and walnuts.

Tokyo, Japan

Foodie heaven with more than 250,000 places to eat and drink including:
traditional, rustic Kobatayaki restaurants (seafood and vegetables cooked
over an open grill); izakaya (Japanese gastro-pubs for sashimi or gyoza
(dumplings); Kanda district's noodle joints and streets dedicated to
okonomiyaki (make-your-own-seafood-pancakes on table-top hotplates);
yakitori stalls (soy marinated grilled skewers); shabu-shabu bars for meat
and fish dipping in a boiling fondue-like clear broth; sukiyaki (thinly sliced
beef cooked in soy, stock and sake broth and dipped in raw egg, served with
tofu, bamboo shoots and other vegetables). Plus Kappabashi-don 'Kitchen
Town' for rechereché utensils.

WHAT TO SAVOUR: Tsukiji: the vast frenetic market on the banks of the
Sumida River where over 450 species of dazzlingly fresh fish pass through
everyday – many of them still alive: yellowtail, bonito, anego (like small
conger eel), sea urchin. Gastro-tourists arrive at 5am for the tuna auction
and breakfast on toro tuna sushi. Special unagi eateries, totally dedicated to
earthy sweet eel (note: flesh and skin eaten); noodle ramen (soba noodles to
slurp with a soy/wasabi sauce).

WHERE TO EAT: Stay overnight in a traditional Ryokan where you sleep
on tatami mats and are served Kaseiki-style exquisitely arranged, strictly
seasonal meals in your room after visiting the hot springs.

WHAT TO BRING BACK: Kitchenware from the Kappabashi-dori
district – especially sieves – including the finest spiders, wooden sushi rice
bowls and knives (though beware the angle on Japanese knives is on one
side only as they use a different cutting technique) and, essential for
Foodies' rice accoutrement, a shamoji – a round spoon made from wood or
bamboo that is traditionally used only to toss and serve rice.

Better Foodie gastro-wanderlust

FULLY-FUNCTIONING BETTER FOODIES HAVE AN INSATIABLE GASTRO WANDERLUST; it's an intrinsic part of our make-up. The siren call of an appetite-quickening seqüência de camarão, a procession of shrimp dishes by the breathtaking Lagoa de Conçeicão on the Brazilian island off Santa Caterina, the country's shellfish mecca, is enough to have the Better Foodie on full epicurious alert, rifling their savings and re-prioritising their must-have gastro-destinations..

ISLANDS HAVE AN INEXORABLE DRAW as they're highly likely to have satisfying ultra-local dishes. Tantalisingly tempting are the Aeolian islands, off the coast of spectacularly Foodie Sicily, and in particular unspoilt Pantelleria, known for its juicy sought-after capers. Appetisingly intriguing, too, is tranquil Maderia, a mélange of Portuguese and Brazilian culinary influences – where Stephane Raimbault is redefining island specialities.

FOR GASTRO-SENSORY OVERLOAD the Better Foodie always relishes an exuberant new street food experience: the snack wallahs of Mumbai with hissing pans of pungent 'wet' bhul, pouches of puffed rice, aromatic dhals and spicy tamarind broths and delicate bamboo-shoot curries or from a hole-in-the-wall Shanghainese vendor divine xiao long bao pork dumplings with scalding savoury broth or xiao long xia, chilli and Sichuan pepper fried crayfish. The Better Foodie is eager to devour Shanghai's revitalised gourmet scene, too: emerging new stars include Jerome Leung at Whampoa Club – refining Shanghainese classics with a luxe twist. Rising in gastro-cool status are edgy modern Turkish/Ottoman eateries in Istanbul, including prime Bosphorus river terrace spot, Muzedechanga, at the Istanbul Modern, serving modish mezze and Ottoman court dishes at Feriye Lokantasi.

Which is generally hotter: Thai green or red curry?

Green is usually hotter as it is based on the green 'Khee noo' chilli, which has a higher scoville rating.

What's the difference between caperberries and capers?

Capers are the pickled flower-buds of a Mediterranean shrub, mainly found in Sicily and the Aeolian islands. Caperberries are the pickled and brined fruit of the same bush.

What are Saturn peaches?

Ambrosial, small, scented, flattened peaches from Italy, which have a very short season from the end of June to late July.

Which region of Italy is buffalo milk mozzarella from?

Campania, close to Naples, particularly the areas around Battipaglia and Caserta. Also conveniently home to San Marzano – special, long-shaped, exceptionally flavoursome tomatoes.

What fruit was the first marmalade made from?

Quince.

What vegetable is the cultivated form of wild cardoon?
Artichoke.

Which British cow's milk cheese is wrapped in nettle?
Cornish Yarg.

Is prosciutto exclusively from Parma?
Absolutely not; many Italian regions have their own prosciutto.
The difference is in the ageing, and the feeding of the pigs
themselves. Prosciutto di Parma is made from pigs that have been
fed on whey – a by-product of making parmigiano reggiano.

**What spice was Cleopatra said to have used on her
complexion, the Greeks strewn their courts with,
and Nero ordered to be sprinkled on the streets of
Rome when he returned victorious from battle?**
Saffron.

What well-known herb family is angelica a part of?
Parsley.

THE FESTIVE
Better
Foodie

The Better Foodie Christmas
beyond the turkey / goose conundrum

Better Foodies are in their element in the build-up to Christmas. Afterall, it's the ultimate opportunity to flaunt discerning proper Foodie prowess. We're the smug yulers, liable to go into ecstatic over-drive with our forward planning and strategic sourcing of definitive ingredients for deeply gastro-memorable meals. We start rum macerating our Christmas pudding vine fruits (richly fragrant Spanish Malaga raisins, golden sultanas, mission figs) several months ahead, having already fished our wild salmon during the summer open season and despatched it for bespoke smoking.

THOUGH THE BETTER FOODIE IS VERY MUCH IN FAVOUR OF
TRADITIONAL FOODS AND FEASTS, their adventurous – not to
mention competitive – streak dictates a temptation to expand their
Christmas culinary boundaries far beyond the eternal turkey/goose
conundrum. Researching alternative Yuletide feasts really gets their gastric
juices flowing and is the perfect excuse for exploring unfamiliar food
shopping territory. It also justifies a brief, sourcing, gastro-break: Pierre
Hermé's marrons glacés from Paris, fresh truffles from Alba, smoked
reindeer from Finland, pickled Baltic herrings from Sweden or a traditional
Lebküchen advent calendar from Nuremberg's Christkindlemarkt.

THE BETTER FOODIE'S HOME EMBRACES SEASONAL EDIBLES
WITH PASSION, PURPOSE AND STYLE: perhaps a Swedish Advent
wreath of braided branches of juniper (a traditional symbol for happiness
and good fortune); an edible bacchanalian still life of pomegranates,
kumquats, quinces, medjool dates, walnuts; or an antique glass tazza
(multi-tiered dish) of sweetmeats (including Spanish turron), Portugueuse
Elvas plums, Turkish delight and Siennese Ricciarelli; orange-laced
amaretti; or a lavish floral display of rosehips, elder, blackberries and sprigs
of scented rosemary.

RECHERCHÉ TRACKLEMENTS are a palate-stimulating passion of the
Better Foodie, however illustrious the cold cuts. We're particularly partial to
the blowsy fruitiness of pickled damsons, arcane pickled walnuts, geranium
jelly and the most distinctive chilli preserves. In recent years, I've bowed to
the preference of my non-carnivorous Better-Foodie-in-the-making son and
served fish: sea bream with Romesco sauce (almond, saffron and peppers),
luxurious turbot in a salt crust with warm caper and fennel dressing, or
Dover sole with creel-caught langoustines and saffron cream.

EVEN IF THE BEST WILD SMOKED SALMON IS NON-NEGOTIABLE, we're likely to serve it with fresh horseradish French crème fraiche and own-made blini or a personalised Poilane loaf adorned with a holly and ivy crust and tailor made message. We may ring the changes with Finnish salted salmon with juniper berries and coriander seeds, an Asian inspired take on gravadlax, potted Morecambe Bay shrimps or grilled langoustine with Seville orange dressing. For many Better Foodies the festivities bring francophile tendencies to the fore and only foie gras or native oysters (kept on, but not swimming in ice, under a damp cloth in the garden shed overnight) will do. A grandiose indulgent Spanish starter is a good alternative, too: cecina (air-dried and gently smoked beef from Castille) served with pine nuts, parmigianno reggiano and a slug of best Nunez de Prado extra-virgin olive oil, or some incomparably aromatic, delicately marbled acorn-fed pata negra from Extremadura.

THE TURKIVOROUS BETTER FOODIE HOUSEHOLD WILL ONLY SERVE A BIRD OF THE HIGHEST WELFARE: extensively free-ranging, organic cereal-fed, slow-growing, traditionally bred, raised to full maturity, dry-plucked by hand and game-hung for a minimum of twelve days to maximise flavour and tenderness. Copas, Kelly Bronze or chapon de Bresse are the choicest birds. Of course, great thought goes into the rigorously Foodie accompaniments: fresh chestnuts laboriously cooked and peeled, cobnuts, pain d'epice, membrillo (Spanish quince paste) and chorizo, or an Arabic pinenut, almond, cinnamon and rice recipe to give favoured Foodie accents to the all-important stuffing – crucial, too is the dry-cured back bacon rolled around the heritage breed pork chipolatas (preferably ritually own-made at the home of a small-holding Better Foodie friend). Tucking slivers of truffle under the bird's skin brings paroxysms of Foodie pleasure to the festive table.

Cheese features prominently in the festive planning.

Aside from a properly affineured (and never scooped from the middle) **Colston Bassett stilton**, we like to proffer several alternative British blues:

Devon blue A cow's milk cheese with fruity and almost caramel and leather nuances.

Harbourne Blue A rich and tangy goat's cheese.

Lanark Blue Unpasteurised, sharp yet creamy, blue-veined ewe's milk cheese.

Cayuga Blue A US alternative. Made from raw goat's milk, this is a blue cheese with a toasty, piquant flavour from the Messmer family's Lively Run Goat Dairy in New York state.

Rogue River Blue A handmade creamy-peppery cow's milk cheese wrapped in grape leaves macerated in Oregon pear brandy.

IF IT REALLY HAS TO BE ROAST POTATOES, THEY MUST BE COOKED IN DUCK FAT. Otherwise: a gratin of Jerusalem artichokes, cardoons and kumera with plenty of nutmeg, parsnip skordalia (a purée of garlic, lemon, oil and breadcrumbs) or recherché black beluga lentils. Sprouts (unless suitably razzed up with preserved lemon, chilli and pistachio), have been jettisoned in favour of brussel tops – the Yule alternative to cime di rapa. As an alternative, try a cross-culture Middle Eastern reference with saffron carrots, star anise and garlic salsify; parchment-wrapped parcels of braised celery, fennel, red onion and rosemary; maple and sesame roast root vegetables; Chinese five-spice red cabbage; mixed braised beets with smoked pancetta or braised chicory in red wine with chestnuts. It's an occasion when the Better Foodie needs a dramatic salad: blood orange, black olives and radish with a few slivers of pickled Japanese ginger, a splash of orange blossom water and a dusting of ground cinnamon.

ONLY THE MOST HARD-CORE BETTER FOODIE VENTURES TO RETURN TO FIFTEENTH-CENTURY SAVOURY MINCE PIES filled with rabbit, pigeon, partridge, dried fruit and spices, but I'll only eat melt-in-the-mouth short mince pies – preferably with the all-important addition of ground almonds in the pastry and fulsomely fruity own-made mincemeat. I'm also partial to Middle Eastern inspired variations with filo pastry and orange flower infused dried fruits, or miniature Santiago tarts with membrillo, citrus zest, almonds and oloroso sherry. Most Better Foodies have a penchant for dark, aromatic, brandied Christmas fruit cake – as long as the dried fruits are of impeccable provenance and the cake is bejewelled with glacé fruits, pecans and marrons glacés, rather than covered in icing. A Better Foodie will doubtless attempt to ring the changes with Danish Julekage, Austrian stollen with dark rum and citrus peel, and Greek walnut and rosewater cake.

GOOSE GASTRONOMES ARE RATHER SUPERIOR ABOUT THEIR PREFERENCE. I actually prefer my goose smoked, as an alternative starter, and would far rather a game bird for smaller festive gatherings: cinnamon rubbed wild duck scattered with pomegranate seeds served with honeyed quince. Alternatively: a rolled haunch of venison, a suckling pig or a fully traceable roast forerib of beef on the bone with bone marrow. The Better Foodie ham is glazed with verjuice, orange, cloves and molasses and served with mostarda di Cremona – piquant single varietal mustard fruits, which are, as Elizabeth David remarked: 'Absolutely original in flavour'.

I ALWAYS CONTEMPLATE FLOUTING CONVENTION COMPLETELY BY GOING WHOLLY VEGETARIAN. I ponder an exquisite Persian pilaf with fragrant dried limes, saffron, pistachio and sweet-sour barberries, with a reddish-gold herby crisp crust, served with a yoghurt, aubergine, walnut and saffron boorani; a Persian sweet and sour ratatouille dish with quince, apple, apricot, aubergine and courgettes, made aromatic with advieh (a mix of dried rose petals, cinnamon, cumin and cardamom seeds) and served with Cypriot chickpea and spinach and flat bread; or a luscious four-mushroom (girolles, chanterelles, cepes and crimini) puff pastry coulibac with cucumber, dill and sour cream sauce.

EVEN BETTER FOODIES WHO ADHERE TO THE SACROSANCT ESSENTIALS MAY JETTISON THE PLUM PUDDING in favour of a Madeiran bolo de mel; an artisan Milanese panettone, preferably served with fresh ricotta and fragrant wild mountain honey; or a festive pandoro (golden Veronese cake) trifle. Being a chestnut fanatic, I've served a delectable River Café marron ice cream and painstakingly made fluffy pyramids of fresh chestnut purée infused with vanilla seeds and anointed with dollops of Jersey whipped cream, for a truly decadent Mont Blanc.

Better Foodies will have a French Christmas Eve Reveillon...

...serving foie gras, oysters, boudin blanc, capon, a bûche de Noël and chocolate mendiants, and they always celebrate Twelfth Night with an almond-rich galette des rois. They're tempted by the full-on feasting of a Polish Wigilia Christmas Eve feast involving twelve courses representing the twelve apostles and including beetroot soup, poppy seed noodles, herring, and carp in aspic; a Scandinavian Christmas Eve smorgasbord with several varieties of marinated herring, gravadlax, baked ham, frikadeller (pork meatballs), smoked reindeer, rice pudding and dried fruits; or a Mexican mole of chocolate, chilli, rosemary and figs.

FOR A TRULY DIFFERENT YULETIDE CENTREPIECE try hallaca –
a mixture of beef, pork, capers, raisins and olives, wrapped in a cornmeal
dough, bound with a banana leaf and steamed as is usual in Venezuela;
Czech carp with a black sauce of damson cheese, pain d'epice, grapes and
almonds; or an Irish Christmas speciality: spiced beef or ox tongue rubbed
with a potent mix of pimento, all spice, cloves, ginger, juniper, mace,
nutmeg and black pepper. A truly robust alternative would be to venture
Guyanese and serve a spectacular cassava-based pepperpot and black
molasses cake, richly spiced and redolent with fruits that have macerated
for weeks in over-proof rum.

OUR FESTIVE CHEESEBOARD DEFINES OUR COMMITMENT TO
THE FINEST AND MORE UNUSUAL CELEBRATORY ALTERNATIVES.
We remain partial to powerful Carles Roquefort and Spanish Picos de
Europa. Blue cheeses should be carefully partnered with slivered fennel,
Zante grapes or ripe pears, toasted walnuts and drunken raisins.

NATURALLY, THE BETTER FOODIE-IN-TRAINING CHILD IS
INVOLVED IN THE EDIBLE FESTIVE PLANNING. They relish making
stained glass biscuits from boiled sweets and sticking cloves into clementines
for the tree. As presents for doting Foodie relatives, Christmas florentines or
squidgy truffles are lovingly, and imperfectly, made. With parental guidance
they can also produce a stunning gingerbread house – naturally with all
Foodie mod cons.

Other celebrations to celebrate foodily
the Better Foodie's Feast Calendar

Better Foodies are highly and hedonistically observant, yet not bound by religious constraints; they're more than happy to dip into all manner of culinarily celebrations of different observances. They can think of nothing better than spending many hours researching, shopping and preparing to celebrate foodily the latest festival they've 'discovered' – the more recondite the better – where abundant, lingering, civilised feasting is involved.

Epiphany Better Foodies fall in with this French celebration with a Galette des Rois butter puff pastry gateau with frangipane. Whoever finds the hidden charm (preferably a bijou Limoge porcelain trophy from Ladurée) is crowned King/Queen for the day and orders everyone around.

Burn's Night The most tenuous Scottish connection is excuse enough for Foodies to celebrate on 25th January. Source the best haggis (sheep's offal, savoury, thyme, mace and cloves) from Edinburgh butcher John Macsween (who makes a vegetarian version with beans and nuts) and serve with bashed neeps, swedes and tatties. Eat Cullen skink (hearty potato soup of undyed smoked haddock) and Scottish cheeses: mild, soft Isle of Mull cheddar, crowdie, preferably Stone's black crowdie (cow's milk curd, rolled in pinhead oatmeal and black pepper) and nutty Cairnsmore, with good rough oatcakes.

Valentine's Day Better Foodies shudder at the mere thought of an evening of heart-shaped commercial tenderness and unseasonal strawberries. We'd rather do a tongue-firmly-in-cheek, pink-hued, luxurious meal at home: pata negra iberico ham and treviso salad; lobster and champagne risotto; forced rhubarb fool; or simply serve aromatic foods of heady aroma.

Shrove Tuesday Better Foodies see this as opportunity to flaunt their considerable batterie of pancake variations. We all enthuse about crêpes suzettes served with suitable pomp – as at The Ritz – but we're equally happy to emulate a Breton crêperie with savoury buckwheat galettes oozing spinach and mature gruyère or Bayonne ham, and cinnamon and apple or marron crêpes. We like to surprise with alternative pancakes: chickpea socca from Nice; Ligurian farinata or Indian dosas; chestnut flour necci from Lucca; tigariki from Crete; buckwheat flour blinis from Russia; Moroccan semolina baghir or ataif (rosewater-spiked Middle Eastern pancakes).

Foodie New Year

Epicurious cosmopolitan Better Foodies spend much of their year marking New Year – after all, there's no better excuse for renewing high Foodie resolutions and for embarking on in-depth entertaining. Choose between:

Oshogatsu The Japanese New Year is customarily celebrated at the end of December/early January. Soba noodles are eaten to see in the New Year and the first meal is ozoni: delicate sticky rice cakes, served in a fish and vegetable mochi broth.

Cap d'Anno See in New Year Italian-style with bollito misto, mostarda and salsa rossa or zampone (pig's trotters) and tiny green 'lucky' lentils.

Chinese New Year Go to town with dim sum, which has to include char siu buns. More traditionally it involves cooking fish (representing abundance and good fortune) and noodles (for longevity), mooli (white radish) pudding with rice flour, air-cured pork and shrimp, or Ken Hom's family recipe of vegetable casserole with bean curd, dried mushrooms, black moss (a Cantonese seaweed) and Shaoxing rice wine. Better Foodie children must be introduced to the delights of sesame coated puffed rice, crushed peanut dumplings and sweet bean paste cakes.

Norooz The Persian New Year is celebrated on the first day of Spring (21st March). Sabzi Polo Mahi (a green herb rice with parsley, coriander, chives, dill, fenugreek and saffron) accompanied by fried fish, and kookoo (a herb omelette) is traditionally eaten alongside sweetmeats, including cardamom-infused chickpea-flour shortbreads shaped as four-leaf clovers.

Enkutatash The Ethiopian New Year is ideal for Better Foodies determined to be different. It is celebrated in September with traditional dishes including kitfo (steak tartare with clarified butter) and dora watt (a fiery chicken stew with hard-boiled eggs eaten from a communal pot) scooped up with injera (a pancake-like bread).

Rosh Hashanah Jewish New Year in the Autumn ranks highly with the Better Foodie, with its strictly seasonal harvest festival overtones. Gefilte fish with beetroot chrain is an acquired taste the Better Foodie is, of course, entirely at home with. (It reminds me of my grandmother, whose poached gefilte fish was peerless, though it did help that my grandfather was briefly a fishmonger.) Carrot tsimmes cooked with honey, apple juice and golden sultanas are the right accompaniment, followed by spiced milk and honey cake or Claudia Roden's Egyptian style pomegranate and roast quince.

Divali Respecting the Hindu New Year and Festival of Light in October, the Better Foodie eats no meat after 6pm. It's the perfect pretext for a flurry of fresh spice roasting and grinding to prepare a spectacular vegetable curry with silky, flaky paratha and pumpkin chutney, potato and chickpea aloo, split-pea dhal, and keer (a sweet rice and milk pudding), which the Better Foodie respects is traditionally served on the same plate as the curry.

St Patrick's Day Better Foodies have a penchant for Irish food and happily mark this day (March 17th) with at the very least a full Irish cooked breakfast – in which black pudding and soda farls are mandatory. They enjoy treating suitably appreciative friends to the very best Irish Belvelly wild smoked salmon with buttermilk bannocks, a slow-cooked Irish stew (strictly no carrots), boxty potato cakes and Irish farmhouse cheeses including: Durrus, Gubbeen and, most recherché, aged Imokilly cheddar, which is only sold in the shop at the legendary Ballymaloe hotel.

Passover Provoking a near frenzy of food-celebration-planning, this is the defining Jewish ritual meal to which I always invite curious and suitably greedy non-Jewish Better Foodie friends. Central is a seder plate (ours was designed by my gastronomically precocious son – a first at our local pottery café) including a roasted lamb shank, as a reminder of the sacrifices made at the temple; parsley – a green herb to symbolise spring; fresh horseradish as the bitter herb used to represent slavery; a roasted egg to symbolise the continuity of life and charoset (a truly delectable paste of fruit and nuts) to symbolise the mortar that was used by the slaves in the construction of the Pharaoh's buildings. It's the start of eight days of eating only unleavened matzah (as there was no time for the dough to rise in the desert when the Hebrews were fleeing). Our ritual meal invariably includes chicken soup with matzo balls (knaidlach in Yiddish), roast chicken or baked black bream with herb sauce, almond cake and dried fruit compote.

Easter Besides single varietal/single plantation chocolate treats, the Better Foodie can't resist a spot of culinary travelling when preparing for Easter. They will eagerly ring the changes with Ligurian Easter pie, or pasteria, (made with spinach, ricotta cheese and eggs) and Columba Pasquale (similar to pannetone, but dove-shaped) from Italy, calcotades (whole small onions that have been grilled over coal) dipped in romesco sauce to accompany a selection of charcoal-grilled meats from Spain, or, more authentically arcane, have a Greek Orthodox Easter with tsoureki (a yeast cake with a blood-red dyed hardboiled egg) for breakfast, aromatic mayeritsa soup (made with lamb offal, lemon, dill and fresh oregano) and roast lamb. The Better Foodie will probably already bake their own hot cross buns or, for something a little bit different, make Cornish saffron buns and will seek out artisan-chocolatier-made fishes or bells for their Foodie-in-the-making children, in homage to the French custom.

Japanese Day-of-the-Ox or Doyo-no-Ushi It's fair to assume that most Better Foodies have a more than a usual penchant for Japanese culinary customs and look forward to this culmination of a two-week long celebration at the end of July. Kabayaki (fresh eel) eating day marks the hottest day of the year (it changes annually according to the lunar calendar), a tradition dating back to the 1600s. The logic behind this custom being that eel boosts the immune system in the heat of summer. Kabayaki are seasoned with sansho (mild, slightly lemon-flavoured pepper) during charcoal grilling basted in mirin, soy sauce and sugar, which caramelises irresistibly.

Michaelmas Celebrated in late September, this occasion is traditionally marked with a roast goose with sage and onion.

Eid This marks the end of Ramadan fasting and is a favourite feast of arch Better Foodie Nigella Lawson. It is more than reason enough to indulge in an ultra-luxurious curry enriched with a delicious combination of almonds and dried fruit, accompanied by spiced pilaf and utterly moreish carrot halwa.

Thanksgiving We may well save ourselves for Thanksgiving – the ultimate Better Foodie festival – as its very purpose is to celebrate feasting. No matter where they are living, November 21st is never missed by the Better Foodie. The larger the crowd the better, especially as it's the perfect excuse to serve a Cajun turducken (an elaborately layered, monumental feast of de-boned turkey stuffed with de-boned duck, in turn stuffed with de-boned chicken plus requisite oyster, andouille and cornbread dressings), alongside the customary sweet potatoes with maple syrup, cornbread and cranberry stuffing, plus pecan and pumpkin pie.

Channukah The Better Foodie is fervently fond of irresistible, crispy yet soft within, potato latkes (pancakes made from finely grated raw potato). The festival (in December) commemorates the second century BC victory of the Jews, led by Judah Maccabee, against the oppressive Syrian ruler, King Antiochus. On reaching the damaged synagogue they had only enough holy oil to last one day but, miraculously, it lasted the eight days it took to fetch more – hence the symbolic lighting of eight candles on the menorah and the eating of fried foods. The Better Foodie treats the festival like a global grazing menu – according to what most appeals – knowing that the Italians eat pollo fritto; Moroccans, couscous with deep-fried chicken; Israelis, ponchkes (jam-filled doughnuts); Greeks, honey-soaked cinnamon pastries, such as loukomades; Egyptian's, zalabia (orange blossom fritters); and is delighted that dishes with curd cheese and sour cream – including cheesecake and cheese blintzes (eggy pancakes filled with vanilla and ricotta) – are essential eating, too.

Better Foodies recognise more bizarre festivals, too

as long as they feed our taste for gatherings around food. We embrace Mexican Day of the Dead picnics, with homemade tamales, corn tortillas, cherished chilli imbued recipes, seasonal salsas and spiced chocolate drinks. Of course Halloween brings out the playful Better Foodie: I'm sure I'm not alone in revelling in planning of a suitably ghoulish, yet delicious, Halloween tea for Better Foodie-in-the-making children with marmite glazed cheese broomsticks, pumpkin and ginger soup, squid ink pasta with blood-red tomato sauce and home-made blackcurrant jelly with peeled lychee or grape eyeballs!

Foodie gifts to give
wrapping up the Better Foodie's present list psyche

Better Foodies are, by their very nature, magnanimous present-givers: they adore any excuse for gastro-shopping for the kitchen, table or, best-of-all, luxuries for the larder, and inevitably succumb to rarely seen, indulgent larder Prada for themselves, too. They excel in instant recall of the best far-flung sources of eclectic edibles and dedicate many enjoyable hours to sourcing and sampling. They take vicarious pleasure in the giving, especially as it's an unwritten rule among fellow Better Foodies to share the spoils.

Adoption of an olive tree, apple tree or vineyard entitling the recipient to a juicy bounty of its spoils and the chutzpah of loftily offering guests their olive oil, apples or wine.

Hunks of aged Parmigiano Reggiano cheese with a traditional Parmesan knife.

Classic Gianduiotti Made from the pure, first pressing of cocoa butter and the finest Piedmont 'tonda' hazlenuts and produced, traditionally, by piping the mixture into little moulds. Having experienced the wondrous and unforgettable aroma of freshly roasted nuts and chocolate at Gobino, one of the best artisan makers, I'm smitten.

A Gift token for a tutored cheese tasting, bread-making or knife skills day.

Membership of Slow Food or another revered Foodie association

Gluttonous Gardener's Pomegranate Box with a young potted tree and bottle of pomegranate molasses.

Chic salad servers for the best-dressed salads.

The recipe lavishly praised at your home, handwritten and wrapped, scroll-like, with an appropriate culinary implement and a stash of the hard-to-source ingredient necessities.

Ultimate tasting box Chloe Doutre Russell's (chocolate buyer at Fortnum & Mason) authoritative chocolate connoisseur's manual and a selection of top bars with tasting notes

Better Foodie stocking fillers
beyond the clementine and wet walnut

I've yet to meet an adult who does not enjoy the nostalgic thrill of their own Christmas stocking; better still a Better Foodie gourmet stocking crammed with a thoughtful mix of the playful, the unexpected and the delectably edible. Shop for culinary curiosities throughout the year in kitchen, junk and charity shops, delis, off-the-beaten-track ethnic speciality emporia and, of course, when on your culinary travels.

Plump, sticky marrons glacés (candied chestnuts) ready-wrapped in shiny gold or silver foil.

A rhizome of fresh ginger Plus a cane ginger grater (from Chinese supermarkets).

A phial of saffron threads and a tiny brass mortar and pestle (from Indian grocers) for pounding the saffron.

Jar of Onuga The SOS (Save Our Sturgeon) alternative to caviar and a mother-of-pearl spoon.

An old-fashion butter curler.

A packet of seeds for unusual salad or herbs for planting in a garden or window box (think mizuna, purple leafed basil, mustard cress).

Silver tea strainer and a packet of single estate tea.

A book bar For that age-old problem of keeping your place in a much-thumbed cook book.

Antique nutcrackers In good working order.

Rose petal syrup A Slow Food Presidia artisanal product in danger of extinction (courtesy of Carluccio).

A dark chocolate spoon for melting into the ultimate, warming hot chocolate (another Carluccio gem).

Smart adjustable measuring spoon For acute accuracy.

A luscious jar of nuts in Acacia honey.

Chocolate snails stuffed with grappa raisins, or fat figs stuffed with candied fruit and walnuts dipped in bitter chocolate

Combination mushroom knife and cleaning brush.

A nutmeg grinder with storage space for several nutmegs (Divertimenti have a particularly svelte well-functioning model).

An oyster knife and the promise of a delivery of a dozen natives.

Gift token for a tutored cheese or chocolate tasting.

A hand-tied bunch of pricey Madagascan vanilla pods.

Home-made Foodie gifts

Rather smug, cost-saving and beatifically well-received. No present, however expensive, can match the pleasure of receiving the tastefully home-made, whether it's fulsomely fruity mincemeat with a hefty Calvados slug; irresistible melt-in-the-mouth smoked paprika dusted cheese straws; an unusual tracklement – quince jelly or chutney; fabulous flavoured oil; salt-pickled lemons in a spruced-up kilner jar to add instant razz to a tagine; old-fashioned fudge made recherché with cocoa nibs; or plump gingerbread-foodies jauntily iced with the recipient's initials in chocolate.

What modish Asian snack literally translates as 'to touch the heart'?

Dim sum.

Who was the author of the earliest recorded cookbook?

Apicus, author of 4AD *De Re Coquinaria*. The first English cookery book was *A Forme of Cury*, written in the late 14th century by Richard II's cook.

What are ormers and where are they from?

Ormers are otherwise known as abalone and are found only in the UK's Channel Islands (Guernsey, Jersey and Alderney). They are hand-fished by wading out neck-high in ice-cold water and feeling for the rare molluscs under brackish weed.

What is often described as the foie gras of the sea?

The creamy liver of a monkfish. Creamy-white with orange tinges, it has the smoothness, richness and texture of duck or goose foie. Good fishmongers will obtain it, on request.

Where in Italy are you most likely to find a pasta dish cooked with sardines?

It's a classic Sicilian dish usually with pinenuts, raisins and saffron.

Where does mustard get its name from?

The 'must', or leftovers, from winemaking; the strained juice was originally added to mustard.

We all know Harry's Bar in Venice is famously expensive, and is where the Bellini was first created, but what classic cocktail was first created in Harry's Bar, Paris, in 1921?

The Bloody Mary.

What are Eccles cakes?

Originating from Lancashire, England, these are made with flaky (often puff) pastry and filled with chopped peel, currants, mixed spice and nutmeg.

What makes vincisgrassi the Better Foodie's ultimate lasagne?

It is made with chicken livers, veal sweetbreads, mushrooms, spices, cream and shavings of truffle.

What spices should be an integral, yet subtle, part of potted shrimps?

Blades of mace, freshly grated nutmeg and a generous pinch of cayenne pepper.

THE INTRICACIES OF
High
Foodism

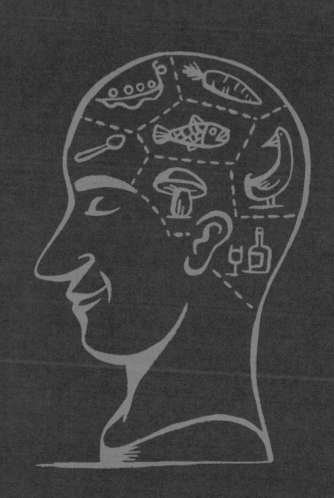

Better Foodie foodementals
core gastro-knowledge for full Foodie credentials

For the fully-fledged Better Foodie – not to mention the gastronaut-in-training – it is not enough to be able to wax lyrical about the most delectable comestibles. It is better still to know how to cook them and, equally crucial for full gastro-credentials, is a connoisseur's understanding of why such foods stand out from their peers, the food tenets that matter, the Foodie myths to be exposed and the solecisms never to be committed.

TO BROWN OR NOT TO BROWN? The controversy is to do with recognising that searing, as recommended in countless books, does not seal in juices. It's important because of the Maillard reaction, which provides 'unami' flavour. When the proteins and sugars in the meat are exposed to high heat (searing) myriad chemical reactions occur, which flavour and brown the meat surface.

WHAT MAKES A GOOD EGG? Eggs are non-negotiable. Better Foodies only buy totally free-range, high-welfare eggs from happy hens with access to plenty of outdoor space, and preferably organic eggs with their plumper yolks, more viscous whites and richer, more eggy taste. Battery hens are laying machines; 'barn eggs' is a euphemism for eggs from a monstrous crammed shed of miserable birds, and are poor quality: the whites are wan and lacking body. Duck egg yolks are rich and creamy, and they make definitive custard, cakes and the best crème brulées – fashionably savoury, imbued with saffron, wasabi or ginger for keep-up-with-the-chefs appeal.

QUAIL'S EGGS. Ensure that they are free-range; better still, organic, as, until recently, most were kept under the worst kind of battery conditions.

CAN OYSTERS ONLY BE EATEN WHEN THERE'S AN 'R' IN THE MONTH? Rock/pacific or giga (as the French call them) cultivated oysters can be eaten all year. Natives spawn in the summer months, which makes their flesh milky and less plump – and less tasty. In the UK there's an ancient act of Parliament to protect them from being fished during their 'closed' season. Better Foodies adore Cochester natives with their distinctive 'bite' and Slow Food 'ark status', but also favour French Pousses en Claire – 'the Kobe beef' of oysters – and more outré: huge Japanese Kumamoto oysters from Wright Brothers, who supply almost every top London restaurant.

WHY WHEY BUTTERS? Pale gold, nutty and mildly cheesy, whey butters are made from the butterfat separated from the curds as a by-product of artisan cheese-making. Parmigiano Reggiano and Montgomery Cheddar whey butters have an acquired, distinctive, farmyard taste. If not whey, pale gold, grassy, milky-sweet hand-made farmhouse butters bought at the farmers' market are the preferred choice of the Better Foodie.

CHEESES ARE SEASONAL, TOO. The taste (grassier, fruitier and more savoury) of traditionally made farmhouse/artisan cheeses can differ drastically, depending on the pastures and the type of natural flora in the air, which vary throughout the year. The Better Foodie distinguishes between Spring and Autumn milk cheeses, and, though it may be ageist, has a marked preference for either the very young or the most mature.

CHOCOLATE IS NOT ALL ABOUT COCOA SOLID PERCENTAGES. More important is the ratio of cocoa solid to cocoa butter, which can render two 70 per cent bars completely different, depending on the recipe of the chocolate-maker. Though chocolate geeks still talk about cocoa percentages, it's terroir and single origin/single plantation chocolates that really matter. The Better Foodie has rarified taste in chocolate – I'd rather have no chocolate than settle for an inferior bar and have been known to chuck away the odd gift box of dubious, no doubt well-intended, high street truffles. I admit to an extravagant taste for Amedei's Porcelena with its delicate floral aromas and spicy red fruit and almond, extremely long-lingering taste nuances – one of the most expensive and venerated chocolates in the world. Newest high chocolatier is Steve de Vries of Colorado whose choco-mission is to recover heirloom cacao hybrids and re-visit the most humble traditional methods of cacao production in pursuit of perfection and a rather different texture and taste.

Why goose fat is better fat

The French Paradox at its best: goose fat has
far less saturated fat than butter and far healthier
mono- and poly-unsaturated fats. It makes for sublime
roast potatoes and other root vegetables, too.

COLD-PRESSING, FIRST PRESSINGS AND OTHER OLIVE OIL MATTERS. It's a question of taste. Unfiltered oils are not necessarily superior; they have a more velvety texture and the slightly cloudy, sediment-in appearance versions may better conjure up bucolic rusticity, but they oxidise faster and should be keep in a cool, dark cupboard. Look out for oils that carry a harvest date. Earlier picked olives deliver a greener more leafy flavour; late-harvest olives have a more autumnal, golden, sweeter taste.

WHAT IS THE JE NE SAIS QUOI MOST CROISSANTS LACK? The crunchy-on-the-outside-fluffy-and-flaky-within croissant must be made with pure butter and strong plain flour (but not OO). It must also be 'turned' at least five times, without incorporating too much gluten (a process of rolling, folding and proving), to achieve the requisite delicate buttery multi-layers.

FLEUR DE SEL V. SEA SALT. Sea salt is better than table salt as it is free from additives to keep the grains from sticking together. Its larger flakes are far more pleasing texturally, too. Fleur de sel reigns supreme as it is hand-harvested only from the uppermost layers of the salt evaporation ponds. Its light grey colour is from natural trace elements and it's lowest in sodium and most delicate in taste. Fleur de sel is slightly moist, so should be served proudly in a suitably special bowl at table rather than in a grinder.

CHILLI CHOW. The Better Foodie is not impressed by extreme heat chillies, but appreciates their different flavour nuances and chooses accordingly. Chillies to know include the mole trinity: pasilla – long, dark and herby with a hint of liquorice and coffee; anchos – wide-shouldered, short with sweet, fruity flavour; and browny/black mulato – deep dried fruit and tabacco flavours. Dried smoked chipotles and slightly tannic yet sweet guajillo (often stuffed) are instantly recognisable to the Better Foodie, too.

WHY FROZEN PEAS CAN BE BETTER THAN 'FRESH' PEAS. Fresh peas become hard and starchy very quickly so unless they're absolutely freshly picked, the frozen are 'fresher' and taste as good in soups and risotti.

TRUFFLE OIL EXPOSED. A victim of not only its own ubiquity, but, frankly, fake. As Giorgio Locatelli maintains, white truffle rots when steeped in olive oil simply doesn't imbue it with feral gorgeousness. Most is made synthetically. Far better to save up for a rare, hedonistic treat of proper white truffle, shaved with reckless abandon.

CHEFS PREFER GELLAN (EVEN TO BRONZE LEAF GELATINE). This is the cheffy ingredient which makes cubes of hot, crispy deep-fried mayo and eggless lemon curd possible. It's a gelling ingredient able to withstand very high temperatures without breaking down crucial molecular boundaries.

FROTH FINESSE. Lower fat milk (it's all to do with the proteins' workings) gives that all-important foamy mouth-fill and the colder the milk the better the froth for cappuccinos.

THE GENTLER WAY TO DISPATCH A LOBSTER. The Better Foodie knows a stressed lobster eats like cotton wool and, in accordance with RSPCA guidelines, puts it in the freezer for at least two hours before cooking in heavily salted boiling water.

PRIZED WILD TURBOT SHOULD HAVE A SEASON. Presently, turbot fishing is allowed in the spawning season – when the fish are full of eggs and the flesh is not so opulently tasty – so stocks are not being naturally replenished with young turbot. Introducing a 'game' season, as with wild salmon or grouse would mean more turbot to go round.

Is fresh pasta always better than dried?

Dried pasta is highly regarded in Italy, as long as it is made with one-hundred per cent durum wheat flour and high in gluten – which the Italians call semola. Look for the Italian phrase: pasta di semola di grano duro. Inexpensive dried pasta, made partly with soft wheat, is more likely to stick together when cooking and its texture is often soft and flabby. Pasta made in northern Italy has added egg (all' uovo) and is more suitable for cream and butter sauces than Southern tomato and olive oil based sauces. Better Foodies know that Tuscan pappardelle is good with meat and game sauces; Ligurian trenette is the pasta to serve with – preferably homemade – pesto; bucatini are like chunkier hollow spaghetti, served Sicilian-style with fresh sardines; malloreddus are Sardinian razor-shell-shaped – often flavoured with saffron and a little chewy; best served with spicy sausage and tomato ragu.

Supermarket 'fresh' pasta uses pasteurised egg, is often pre-frozen and simply doesn't have the silky texture of made-that-day fresh egg pasta.

WHAT'S THE DEAL WITH RAW UNPASTEURISED MILK? A rare Better Foodie treat, only available at farmers' markets or at the farm gate; equally elusive and ambrosial is rich, almost farmyardy raw, untreated cream.

WHY SUSTAINABILITY MATTERS IN SARDINE TINS, TOO. The Better Foodie seeks out Spanish day-boat, line-caught tinned sardines (Ramon Bue are impeccable calibre). They are plumper, more flavoursome and reach the tins in better shape than indiscriminately trawled sardines.

GALANGAL AND GINGER ARE NOT INTERCHANGEABLE. Galangal has paler flesh and reddish brown skin and is decidedly more peppery.

MAKING SENSE OF MOLECULAR GASTRONOMY. The term was invented by French chemist Hervé This. It simply means applying scientific principles to cooking. The world's pioneers of molecular gastronomy are Ferran Adria of Spain's El Bulli and Heston Blumenthal of The Fat Duck – who disarmingly talks of his 'simple curiosity'. Working with leading scientists, besides having their own kitchen labs, they thrive on understanding complementary molecular structures of unlikely ingredients; questioning and re-interpreting culinary techniques once set in stone. Be wary of wannabe alchemist chefs getting carried away with liquid nitrogen savoury meringues, jellies and espumas without really understanding why.

WHAT GIVES MUSTARD ITS HEAT? When liquid is added to crushed mustard seeds (or powder) it activates volatile mustard oils, which release an enzyme compound called isothiocyanate (also found in horseradish and wasabi root), which gives mustard its characteristic pungent bite. Its name, from the Latin 'burning must', dates back to the Romans who would add unfermented grape juice or must (now called verjuice) to mustard seeds.

PARSLEY INVERTED SNOBBERY. Most self-respecting Foodies have banished curly parsley from their kitchen, but the younger leaves actually have a fuller flavour than the fashionably flat, and are far superior for sauce vierge/salsa verde.

WHY MUTTON IS ENJOYING A RENAISSANCE. Good mutton from a properly bred, raised and grazed sheep and more than two years old (best breeds are Scottish Blackface and North Country Cheviot) needs to be hung for at least two weeks and works best when slow-roasted, poached or in an Irish stew (no carrots). Its revival has been spear-headed by Prince Charles – nostalgic, perhaps, for the mutton of his childhood – but also to help the incomes of hill sheep farmers. Its meat has a complex, intense, savoury depth of flavour and makes much Spring lamb seem innocuously mild and sweet by comparison.

WHAT'S THE DIFFERENCE BETWEEN BLACK, GREEN AND WHITE TEAS? Black tea comes from leaves that have been naturally oxidised after initial drying and fermenting – purest examples are Darjeelings, Assams and Earl Greys, and come from single tea estates in India, Sri Lanka, China and Japan. Green tea leaves are steamed but not fermented. Oolong teas are only partially fermented and lighter in colour, aroma and taste than black, but more robust than green. Most delicate of all are the white teas; Royal White Silver Needles are picked only on two days of the year at dawn and processed entirely by hand.

PRAWN PURCHASING POWER. The committed Better Foodie is wary of warm-water prawns; their farming is well known to be destroying mangrove forests – not to mention racking up air miles and contributing to their vapid taste. Cold water North Atlantic prawns can be enjoyed with integrity.

WHAT'S THE DIFFERENCE BETWEEN PANCETTA AND BACON?
Both bacon and pancetta are from pork belly; pancetta is salt cured,
flavoured with herbs and spices and air-dried.

THE CASE FOR SPELT. Wheat allergy-free and with a nutty taste and
barley-like aroma, it makes delicious bread and pasta.

DO PINK PEPPERCORNS REALLY EXIST? Pink peppercorns are the
berries from a bush that is related to the rose – not a pepper. Culinary
rumours are rife that the pink peppercorn's fruity piquancy (a key Foodie
feature of the late eighties) is due for a comeback. Better Foodies always
offer a choice of freshly purchased peppercorns to suit the dish (Malaysian
Sarawak; chocolate brown, aromatic Tellicherry from the Malabar coast of
southwest India; or citrussy Vietnamese) and they will ensure that their
grinder does coarse.

WHY STOCK MATTERS. All Foodies are fanatical about making their
own stock; its intensity is incomparable and, once a habit is established, it
becomes a fact of life. In preference, ask a butcher for extra bones or save
chicken wings from a bought-to-roast-bird, as the roasted bones add
immeasurably to the flavour. The same goes for langoustine shells, which
make a particularly fine base for a bouillaibasse.

TUNA TRUTHS Always buy line-caught tuna. The only way to serve a
salade nicoise is with fresh-seared tuna. Better foodies adore toro – the
prized belly of tuna, which makes superb sushi. Bonito is always line-caught
and fished by day-boat – it is delicate and pale in colour; yellow fin is
slightly pinker and stronger in flavour. Line-caught ventresca is the only
acceptable tinned tuna, pricey enough to be a treat.

WHAT MAKES STONEGROUND FLOUR BETTER? Whether white or brown it still has the wheatgerm and the flour's natural oil, which makes for better pastry and scones.

TEABAGS: THE FOODIE SOLECISM. There are ten different quality grades of tealeaf. The most popular branded teabags are from the lowest grade, known as 'fannings dust' – a myriad blend of lower quality African teas. An exception is Robert Wilson's exquisite hand-rolled teabags.

CAN VEGETARIANS TRULY BE BETTER FOODIES? Though some die-hard chefs may disagree, vegetarian Better Foodies are surely only making a choice about eating foods which have a benign effect on animal welfare and global issues. They generally care at least as passionately about foods of good provenance (in season and local) and can be as open-minded as any carnivore about culinary travelling.

THE IMPORTANCE OF UMAMI. All self-respecting Better Foodies have been talking about the fifth taste sensation (after salty, sweet, sour and bitter) for years. Simply, it's that moreish savoury-ness found in the pan 'goo' of roast chicken, soy sauce or parmesan. The most forward-looking chefs are introducing it into desserts.

PERTINENT POTATO PARLANCE. Jersey Royals are the only PDO (Protection of Designation of Origin status) spuds – fully traceable to their farm of origin. They have an incomparable nutty, firm texture and flaky cook-in skins.

'It is good food, not fine words, which keeps me alive.'

Moliére, seventeenth-century French playwright.

The Foodemental issues
how to have your ethics and eat them

The Better Foodie's gastro-superiority goes far beyond tasty eating.
We pride ourselves on being fanatically Foodie with a conscience and shoals
of compassion (which means eschewing vulnerable foods however gourmet).
We're rigorously responsible about consuming ethically: our culinary
repertoire rests on carefully produced food-promoting biodiversity and
sustainability with a respect for tradition, terrior and specialist skills. We're
bordering on evangelical about local sourcing, regional gems, and fairtrade,
insisting farmers' markets and box schemes are part of our everyday litany.

Is EATING ORGANICALLY IMPERATIVE FOR THE BETTER FOODIE?
Organic doesn't necessarily equate with better taste. By definition it means
foods produced as 'naturally' as possible – without artificial fertilisers or
insecticides, guaranteed free of GMO (Genetically Modified Organism)
ingredients and in accordance with proscribed sustainability and animal
welfare principles (the Soil Association in the UK). Environmentally,
organic farming naturally promotes biodiversity, enriches the soil and
encourages wildlife. The Better Foodie knows, however, that other variables
(in particular where and when the food is produced) matter, too; an
'organic' Kenyan bean (which makes high demands on precious water and
uses up airmiles) will never taste as good as a home-grown 'heritage' runner
bean. So, it's a question of discriminating as to when eating organically
truly makes a difference. Buying organic potatoes and preferably all root
vegetables, plus celery and spinach is important, as their non-organic
alternatives consistently carry higher levels of pesticide residue. Otherwise,
local, fresh and seasonal is good enough, and often tastier for the Better
Foodie. Concerned Foodies should, in preference, buy organic milk and
other dairy products, eggs, poultry and meat, unless they're in absolutely
no doubt of their impeccable provenance and husbandry.

WHY DO RARE BREEDS MATTER? Better Foodies are currently talking
a great deal about rare-breed meats. This doesn't mean pedigree breeds are
about to become extinct – quite the reverse – they're undergoing a much-
needed revival. Their slow growth and wholly natural diet require great
commitment from the farmer, but this is well worth the effort as the meat
produced is far superior in taste and quality. Whether dining at a fellow
Foodie's house or at a restaurant, the Better Foodie expects to know
whether his chop is Middle White or Gloucester Old Spot, name-checking
its breed, and continually revising their mental gourmet address book.

LOCAL V. FOOD MILES (The distance food travels from field to plate.)
Eating locally and seasonally are by-words for the committed Better Foodie
who is conscious of the detrimental effects of carbon dioxide emissions
contributing to climate change, and the importance of sustaining their
local food communities. Besides the taste (and nutritional) benefits of
freshly-picked produce, the animals are generally less stressed as they
haven't been hauled across the country to centralised abattoirs. Although
we're satisfied to be fully subscribed box scheme fruit and veg. regulars
(we believe produce shouldn't even travel around our country unnecessarily,
see page 235), we're not po-faced purists. We enjoy the occasional exotic
fruit we simply can't grow in our climate, but we only buy in season. It's far
more satisfying to look forward to the first Indian Alphonso mangoes rather
than crave inferior, luscious-lacking fruit all year round.

WHY WILD CAVIAR IS NO LONGER ACCEPTABLE. The export of
wild sturgeon roe has been suspended until producers agree to practice
sustainable fishing methods – not to mention calling a halt to smuggling
and over-fishing. Ever-increasing water temperatures and pollution are also
partly to blame for the sturgeon's rapid decline. The fishing and export
suspension includes the Caspian region, which accounts for ninety per cent
of caviar production, and this may well become a permanent ban. Wise
Better Foodies already prefer smaller, blacker, more briny-fragrant sevruga,
which is far preferable from an environmental point of view. Many have
also switched to farmed caviar – particularly Prunier's Caviar d'Aquitaine
(though true caviar connoisseurs argue that it lacks certain nuances of its
wild counterpart). In the US, eco-friendly home-grown eggs are an
affordable alternative. Classic caviar etiquette of using a mother of pearl
spoon still holds true for farmed caviar, though – no Better Foodie wants a
metallic taste to tarnish their enjoyment.

Fairtrade

This guarantees a minimum price to otherwise
marginalised smaller producers. It is impossible to
denigrate in principle, but as with 'organic' – which
has been adopted by mega-food businesses – some of
its credentials have become diluted. When every coffee
carries a 'Fairtrade' moniker, the Better Foodie becomes
cynical and when in doubt reverts to smaller, more
accountable companies, such as Union Coffee Roasters.
Taste is often compromised, too – much 'fairtrade'
chocolate simply uses inferior African cocoa
beans. Non-negotiables, however, are Fair
Trade Windward bananas, mangoes
and pineapples.

Is veal ever acceptable?

A brief, but good life is surely better than pointlessly
destroying unwanted young dairy calves at birth.
Source British veal that has been well bred in large
barns and that has ideally been fed organically on its
mother's milk and grass. Rose rather than milk-fed
veal is fed on mainly grain and straw
and has darker, less delicate flesh.

BOX SCHEMES Buying directly from the producer means that the food is likely to be ultra-fresh and seasonal. There may be several weeks of purple sprouting broccoli or a glut of asparagus, but the Better Foodie happily (and ever so slightly smugly) revels in seasonal obsessions and will settle into a frenzy of pickling, preserving and sauce-making.

ARE WE FISHING IN THE RIGHT WATERS? The enlightened Better Foodie first became aware of over-fishing/sustainability issues whilst wrestling with his cod consciousness. Even though it is on the endangered list, North Atlantic cod is still acceptable and in the Shetlands the first rigorously aquaculture-approved cod farm provides an alternative. The MSC (Marine Stewardship Council) seal of approval is vital, as is looking out for, and requesting, only fish caught by day-boat in local waters, practising responsible pole-and-line methods. It's not only which fish to eat, but also those less wastefully caught: the number of by-catch fish caught in nets when fishermen are after other species is very high. Better Foodies are already varying their fish habits to include more locally caught fish: megrim sole is fast moving up the gastro-barometer. Farmed fish is beset with problems and depends on the level of aquaculture. Only by sourcing those farmed in open sea conditions can we ensure that they are not being fed on large supplies of wild-caught fish feed! Go for megrim sole, gurnard (a sea bass substitute), mackerel, pollack, Dover and lemon sole, black bream, red mullet, ocean perch, spider crab, halibut, weaver (a good monkfish alternative despite its fearful spines). Cod should be Alaskan or Icelandic; dolphin-friendly yellow-fin tuna, line-caught; ditto the occasional treat of wild sea bass, prawns and langoustines from the North Atlantic. On the environmental watch list are cod, haddock, hake, halibut, monkfish, plaice, shark, skate and warm water prawns from Southeast Asia. For the latest updates on sustainability and related issues visit: www.fishonline.org.

IS FOIE GRAS THE NEW FUR HEADING FOR EDIBLE EXTINCTION? Certainly the very idea of gavage sounds barbaric, but the question revolves around whether the ducks or geese feel the pain of force-feeding. French producers maintain that the birds would naturally eat huge quantities of food before migrating, that they don't have a gag reflex and cite tradition in their favour. For the Better Foodie with a taste for incomparably unctuous silky foie gras, the compromise is to buy only from small artisan producers who are most likely to treat their flocks with care. It's never worth buying tins of bloc de foie gras, however temptingly packaged: this is machine-minced liver pressed together. Parfait must only have twenty-five per cent foie gras, plus added chicken liver or foie gras fat, and paté is a minimum fifty per cent foie gras, made from bloc, surrounded by forcemeat. Better Foodies know only foie gras d'oie entier is made with whole lobes. Shamelessly, I'd rather fresh foie gras or not at all.

Biodynamic farming

Far beyond mere organics, this is based on the
'spiritual science' teachings of Rudolf Steiner, dating
back to 1924. It goes considerably further in terms of
integrating animal, soil and plant to the point of being
completely self-sustaining and entirely traceable.
Biodynamic farms not only produce their own animal
feed, bedding, manure from their own livestock, and
herbal remedies, but take a widely holistic approach,
considering the position of the planets and phases of
the moon to determine when to plant and harvest
crops, with the aim of restoring life to the soil
and being utterly seasonal.

Why the Better Foodie is happy to pay more
foodemental differences they don't always tell you

It almost makes us seem smugly ascetic but the properly committed Better Foodie would rather go without than settle for second best: whether it is bread of dubious texture, cheese of uncertain provenance or – my absolute bête noir – chocolate of indiscriminate cocoa beans and country of origin. We never rate style over substance. We appreciate the finely tuned difference in the slow-reared, artisan produced, impeccably, eco-gastronomically sourced, and take vicarious pleasure in encouraging Better Foodies-in-the-making to taste the difference.

Dry-cure bacon v. cheap bacon When frying dry-cured bacon none of that white scummy liquid will appear in your pan; properly cured pork has the water drawn out of it, whereas water is put back into cheap bacon to up its weight.

Buffalo v. cow mozzarella Quiveringly soft, porcelain-white buffalo has a fragile, loose texture and is, intriguingly, faintly acidic, with a distinct grassy-farmyard taste. Those made by hand have a tell-tale hand tear mark on their outer edge. Better Foodies know the best delis that have fresh buffalo delivered daily. Cow's mozzarella is firm yet bouncy tasting of very little.

Carnaroli v. arborio rice Carnaroli was developed by a Milanese rice grower, who crossed Vialone Nano risotto rice (best for seafood) with a Japanese strain. It makes for a distinctive nuttier, more velvety and creamier tasting risotto, which retains some all-important bite.

Diver caught scallops They are in better condition and are naturally plumper than their dredged counterparts, and are caught without damaging the seabed.

Aged Parmigiano Reggiano v. standard Parmigiano/Grana Padano Only cheese that has been aged for twelve months can be called Parmigiano Reggiano, but is still considered immature. After two years it is considered stravecchio, or very mature. The best are aged for three years under bank vault-like security. More mature Parmigiano Reggiano is crumblier, has a deeper, fruitier and nuttier taste – reminiscent of figs and walnuts – and is better still dribbled with true tradizionale balsamic vinegar. Despite what its producers would tell you, grana padano may be geographically close, but is very much the inferior relation.

Untreated cream v. pasteurised cream Fanatical Foodies in greedy pursuit of purity adore cream made from untreated (non-pasteurised) milk – usually only found at farmers' markets – with its distinctly farmyard richness. It is best splurged on for adorning a seasonal fruit pie, rather than used in cooking.

Jersey Royals v. other 'name' potatoes, including La Ratte and Yukon Gold Their distinctive firm waxy texture and slightly, nutty, earthy, sweet taste is uniquely attributable to Jersey's particularly rich soil and temperate climate. The only potato with PDO 9 (Protected Designation of Origin) Status and impeccable provenance (a Better Foodie mantra), each and every Jersey Royal can be fully traced back to its farm of origin.

Well-aged hung meat v. supermarket meat cuts Meat needs to be hung to develop flavour. Enzymes are produced, which eat away at the muscle fibre, breaking it down and making it tender. It has better fat marbling, too.

Organic chicken v. lesser poultry It's mostly to do with their standard of life. Well-exercised, 'happy' chickens with plenty of freedom and good feed taste better, but the breed has to be right, too. Poulets de Bresse are fed on a 'secret' grain mix and reign supreme, although they are not organic. UK-reared Poulets Anglais are similarly superior.

North European/Breton lobster v. North American/Maine lobster North European lobster is violet-blue when uncooked; North American is brownish-green. Better Foodies prefer the smaller, slower growing north European lobster, which they are convinced has a better-developed flavour.

Poilâne sourdough

Steam-cooked in wood-fired ovens,
costly Poilâne loaves have a mesmerising
crust, earthy, addictive, tangy sourness and are
naturally leavened with wild yeasts using a sour
starter and made with only stone-ground, sifted
wheat flour including a high percentage of spelt
(an old-fashioned grain), water and Guerande
sea salt from Brittany – Poilâne
loaves last longer, too.

When we no longer have good cooking in the world, we will have no literature, nor high and sharp intelligence, nor friendly gathering, no social harmony

Marie-Antoine Carême, French chef of kings – often accredited as the founder of haute cuisine.

Tarbais v. haricot for cassoulet Tarbais are the purist's choice for cassoulet. I remember southwest French chef, Christian Delteil, pouncing, with undisguised glee, on a stall selling fresh tarbais, on a visit some years ago to gather an insider's view on cassoulet from his 80-year-old mother. Genuine tarbais are harvested one pod at a time in the Pyrenees, and are prized for their sweet, mild flavour, silky texture and the way they hold their shape.

Why freshly carved back fillet of smoked salmon is superior Sliced to order, the flesh invariably remains moister. The back fillet is the leanest, most tender part of the fish.

Unsalted French, proper farmhouse and whey butter v. non-Better Foodie ordinary butters By law French unsalted butter (the instinctive Better Foodie choice) has to be more than eighty-two per cent butterfat – hence its high epicurean status and the favouritism shown to intensely buttery Lescure and Echire. Also recommended are the US equivalents, such as Plugra. Provenance, too, is a Better Foodie mantra and we love to buy hand-made, intensely creamy, almost caramely butters at farmers' markets (most pleasingly alongside cream and cheeses from the same producer). Otherwise, we choose artisanal butters from Ronny Brook Farm Dairy in upstate New York or whey butters from favoured cheese producers, such as Montgomery cheddar.

Are jarred roast artichokes and other antipasti ever worth their price? Even the Better Foodie takes shortcuts sometimes and likes to have a stash of emergency delicacies. They are not, however, seduced by flattering labels and will only buy those bottled in proper extra-virgin olive oil – with the tipico taste left in.

Gastro memberships every Better Foodie subscribes to

associations for the voraciously committed

Gregarious as well as discriminatingly greedy, the Better Foodie enjoys nothing more than savouring delectable conversation with their fellow Foodies. They embrace memberships which widen their epicurious network, generally providing food for thought and broadening their gastro-boundaries. They believe, too, in supporting suitably Foodie organisations to further true food values – whether dedicated to food education, eco-gastronomy, sustaining our epicurean heritage or chartering pioneering gastro-intellectual territory.

Slow Food This non-profit organisation has over 80,000 members who meet in convivia or local groups throughout the world. Better Foodies unequivocally share Slow Food's holistic, non-preachy belief in enjoying and learning from the pleasures of good eating. Not only is the Better Foodie an active member of their local group (attending workshops and tastings with acclaimed artisan producers on gastro-essentials from chocolate and culatello to verjuice), but plans gastro-breaks around international events – most notably the biannual Salone di Gusto in Turin – the most deliriously epicurean event in the Foodie's calendar – and the Cheese Festival in Bra.

James Beard Foundation Devoted to celebrating, preserving and furthering the practise of the culinary arts of the US. Membership is a high priority for New York Foodies, who attend workshops and lunches regularly and enjoy the insider's information afforded by the newsletter.

Gardens Organic (formerly HDRA) This protects and researches heirloom vegetables and runs workshops and gardens. Whilst the Victorians had 120 varieties of tall garden pea – which meant continuous supplies all summer – commercial food processors prefer a single variety, which ripen together. Garden Organic has set out to rescue varieties such as Ne Plus Ultra from extinction. Better Foodies relish the idea of doing their bit to save a Bowland Beauty broad bean, Egmont Gold carrot or Whippersnapper tomato, and members can adopt a vegetable!

Seventypercent This began as a website dedicated to proper chocolate, offering detailed and insightful comparative tastings, a chocopedia and chocolate news, besides the means to purchase 'hard-to-track-down' bars from smaller artisan producers. It now runs monthly chocoscenti evenings to taste and discuss fine chocolate and meet the makers.

Foodie New York City based, this is both a blog and a club. 'Members' are invited by founder Joe DeSalazar to attend bi-monthly tasting dinners, on crucial Foodie themes, in loft spaces around the city.

Culinary historians of New York An opportunity for the historically minded Better Foodie with a taste for the esoteric to mix with chefs, anthropologists, food writers and collectors over scholarly workshops, tastings and field trips. Subjects are as varied as a history of the hottest cuisines, the history of pigs and the impact of restaurant reviewing on the New York restaurant scene.

eGullet

Arguably the most highly regarded international Better
Foodie website, only 'members' can participate; the rest
merely gorge on culinary eavesdropping. Fabled author
Paula Wolfert enlisted egullet members for feedback on
a new edition of her iconic food-book on southwest
France. Anthony Bourdain and many other gastro-
luminaries are active members.
(www.egullet.com)

Iconic pilgrimages

tables to salivate over and, blow-the-expense
and waiting list, to try at least once

We know it's bordering on the fanatical, not to mention gastro-geeky, but
the truly committed Better Foodie has a mental wish-list of iconic
restaurants that they aspire to make a pilgrimage to, at least once in their
lifetime. Blow the expense or difficulty in getting there, not to mention the
machinations and intense negotiations necessary to secure a reservation, the
determined Better Foodie will plot and plan and considers no restaurant
too far…

L'Atelier du Robuchon, Paris, Tokyo, New York, London
Such is Joel Robuchon's legendary reputation for extreme culinary
perfection he's habitually referred to as the best chef on the planet – even
among the most hardboiled critics. Robuchon famously closed his three star
temple to haute cuisine in Paris to retire, only to reinvent himself as the
forerunner of the 'bistronomique' – the highest echelon gastro-bistro.
Influenced by tapas and sushi bars, the sublime tasting menu of 'greatest
hits' is a must, including chestnut soup with foie gras, a shot of poached
egg, wild mushrooms and cream; sea scallop with truffle butter; and quite
perfect Poulet de Bresse.

Le Quartier Francais, Western Cape, South Africa Margot
Janse's Tasting Room at a refined auberge in a French Huguenot enclave of
the Cape winelands. She creatively and rigorously seasonally blends French,
Malay and South African influences into thought-provoking Better Foodie
tasting menus: wild mushroom spätzle with poached duck egg and truffle
froth; crayfish ravioli with wilted lettuce, garlic purée, olive and vanilla
foam; paprika-cured Impala loin with cumin scented aubergine; and saffron
custard with honey fruits.

E Bulli, Girona Probably the hardest to book restaurant in the world,
it's only open for dinner April-September. The Catalonian pilgrimage is
non-negotiable: the Better Foodie must experience first-hand the ultimate
in irreverent and innovative haute gastro-couture, where staff always
outnumber diners. Each season eighty new dishes are created. The 26-course
tasting menu, that changes daily – some mere bites or pops – encapsulates
this tour de force, plus a few from 'the archive': parmesan marshmallow
and electric milk; soft boiled quail egg with crisp caramel crust; and melon
caviar are surrealism for the palate.

Bukhara, New Delhi Better Foodies adore the intensity of flavour and the drama of cooking in clay tandoori ovens, and are suitably blown away by dining at the cave-like Bukhara. We highly approve of being encouraged to eat with our hands (whilst wearing bib-like napkins); messy eating is very Better Foodie. Tiny mutton chops with cloves and cinnamon drizzled with saffron; whole shoulder of lamb marinated in vinegar and black cumin; pomfret with paneer are experiences to relish.

Le Manoir Aux Quat Saisons, Oxfordshire, UK Indefatigably passionate Raymond Blanc lives the chef's plot-to-plate utopia. The bucolic and ultra-spoiling hotel/restaurant is surrounded by the most stunning gardens/potagers including the UK's most adventurous Asian vegetable collection. Better Foodies aspire to combine the state-of-the-art cookery school with the full menu gourmand splurge: poached brill with wasabi and scallop agnolotti; corn-fed squab with coco beans and chanterelles; earl grey chocolate tart.

Cal Pep, Barcelona This is the iconic, manic (there is no menu; pointing is de rigeur) tapas bar – a favourite of Ferran Adria, and the inspiration for London's Fino. Incomparable seafood includes tiny chiperones with garbanzos (squid with chickpeas); tallarines (wedge clams); langoustines a la plancha; and botifarra (Catalan sausage with beans). Finish with foam shots of crema catalana.

Pierre Gagnaire, Paris Wildly creative and intellectual, Gagnaire's three-star risk-taking menu is always evolving, which leaves the fanatical Better Foodie craving more. His complex menus require fulsome creation and often involve one ingredient treated in several ways. His progressions of petite puddings – especially the chocolate – are truly memorable.

Once there we request fabled dishes

We feel no compunction about asking for those long-hankered-afer dishes, even if off menu (surely acceptable Foodie code for how seriously we take our dining). Such pursuits definitely bring out the inner collector in the Better Foodie (we always ask for a menu to add to our growing stash). We can't help a certain amount of acquisitiveness in terms of hankering after those most talked about, purr-inducing, pure Foodie taste experiences. We even enjoy them vicariously, and will happily engage fellow Better Foodies who've already notched up a visit to a hallowed dining room in detailed course-by-course savouring. We gleefully, if surreptitiously, congratulate ourselves when we can tick off a good number of definitive dinners in any respected gastro-journal 'best of the world' list.

Michel Bras, Laguiole, France The apogee of back-to-nature, pared down three-star cuisine, using rare 'forgotten' vegetables and herbs growing wild in the Auvergne – absolutely in tune with Better Foodie sensibilities. The view from the startling modern building is part of the aesthetic. Gargoillou is probably the greatest vegetable dish: more than 30 poached separately with extraordinary multiple textures and encapsulating Bras' philosophy. Better Foodies also order poached galloise blanche chicken with aligot and his much-imitated molten chocolate cake.

Jiro, Tokyo Tucked away in the metro subway, the tiny but exquisitely formed Jiro takes the preparation of sushi and its rice to dizzying heights of perfection (reputedly every grain of rice has been counted!). According to chef Joel Robuchon, it redefines all notions of how the ultimate sushi should taste: the sea urchin, toro tuna marinated in soy sauce for precisely fifteen minutes, and pearl hued turbot are peerless.

Manresa, Santa Cruz, California Absolutely in the vanguard of the most inventive and dextrous California cuisine, with influences from Spain, France and Japan (the fish is mostly from Tokyo's fabled Tsujiki market), David Kinch's intelligent, playful, matchless technique is truly revelatory. Even the 26-course tasting menu never stays static: sea scallop with bottarga watercress risotto; shellfish and almond gratin; oyster and sea urchin in a sea water gelee; wild mushrooms and foie grass en papillote with slow-poached egg.

Da Fiore, Venice Family-run paean to seafood, both earthy and refined, lauded by Marcella Hazan. Dishes the Better Foodie desires include turbot consommé; asparagus and parmigiano custard; red mullet with fresh figs and mint; and Venetian lagoon seasonal speciality: moeche (baby crab).

Tetsuya Wakuda, Sydney Ever craving thrilling innovative culinary experiences, the Better Foodie will adore Tetsuya's fusion of Australian and Japanese ingredients, treated with haute French culinary prowess and served on exquisite bespoke 'fusion' ceramics. The dégustation menu transports with silky confit of Petuna Tasmanian ocean trout (from the world's purest waters) with fennel and daikon; roasted baramundi with bitter greens and truffled peaches; grilled fillet of veal with wasabi and sea urchin butter; orange and black pepper sorbet with honey.

French Laundry, California Ultra-sophisticated and technically perfect Thomas Keller's Californian/French cuisine pays fanatical attention to ingredient provenance of the highest order. Sweet butter-poached Maine lobster with pea shoot salad; 'tongue in cheek' cheese desserts and delectable amuses make for a near-perfect Better Foodie experience.

Restaurant Gordon Ramsay, London Intimate, cosseting haute French in London – though sightings of the celebrity chef are far from guaranteed. Every Better Foodie wants to have an opinion on whether the cuisine (tortellini of lobster with vinaigrette crustacea and herb velouté; carpaccio of venison with truffle cream) is as superlative as the hype.

Chez Panisse, California One of the most influential American chefs of all time, Alice Water's supra-Foodie mantra of simply prepared, local, well-sourced seasonal produce was, shockingly, outrageously radical in the early 1970s. Her commitment remains undiminished and her menus extraordinarily evocative and inviting: Hog Island oyster ragout; grilled Cattail Creek Ranch lamb with juniper berry sauce, potato and sorrel gratin and Cannard Farm mâche; and Sierra Beauty apple crisp with Meyer lemon.

Le Louis XV, Alain Ducasse, Monte Carlo

This is the pinnacle of de luxe dining upstaged by superlative ingredients. Humble and earthy Mediterranean ingredients are raised to the sublime in jaw-dropping, sumptuous surroundings. Menus are divided into The Vegetable Garden, The Sea and The Farm. Divine asparagus with tiny, mountain morels, rare San Remo gamberi of complex sweetness, wild seabass a la plancha with raw and cooked Italian violet artichokes, milk-fed Pyranean lamb with hints of cardamom, squab pigeon with truffled liver and chard, hot wild strawberries on icy mascapone sorbet. And the most mesmerising bread and cheese trolleys. Numerous chefs rate it as their most memorable culinary experience ever. Indisputably a must on every Better Foodie's 'to visit' list – bank balance notwithstanding.

Can Fabes, San Celoni, near Barcelona Self-taught Catalan chef and three-star long timer, Santi Santamaria, doesn't court publicity, yet the wood-beamed restaurant/hotel/bistro in Montsera National Park close to Barcelona is a gem: prawn ravioli with cep oil; pigeon with duck tartare; and hare en croute with coco beans are masterly and wholly memorable.

Echaurren, Ezcaray Besides the established classics, the Better Foodie aspires to keep ahead and claim a pioneering experience with the next generation of iconic chefs. Fourth generation family-run in an arcaded and timbered ski-resort the traditional Riojan menu is overseen by mater in one dining room and son Francis Paniego's trail-blazing vanguardia cuisine in the other. Oysters with baked squash purée; Iberian ham ice cream with tomato seeds; Iberico croquetas of exquisite lightness; stunning-textured merluza confitada, deep fried and poached.

The Fat Duck, Bray, UK Light years ahead, Heston Blumenthal's culinary frontier-defining curiosity is insatiable. Besides his fabled snail porridge, sardines on toast sorbet and playful deconstructed childhood sweets, his current preoccupation is with the emotion of dining. His fascination with molecular gastronomy is apparent in the pure pleasure of definitive classic and historical dishes, as in his fun and adventurous dégustation menus.

Masa, New York Temple to rarified sushi where legendary Masa Takayami really is behind the bar preparing an omakase (translates as 'chef, I'm in your hands' experience – there's no written menu – Takayami has a 'black book' to record what each customer eats and their reactions), which may include blissful white truffle tempura in season; aja mackerel in shiso blossom; kobe beef sukiyaki; shabu shabu of lobster; and foie gras, barely poached in broth and dipped in tosazu (vinegar and soy) sauce.

The Better Foodie scholar
esoteric food for thought: chartering deliciously provocative intellectual terrain

The Better Foodie, consciously or not, undertakes a life-long commitment to furthering their culinary knowledge and understanding. For many, it's sufficient to expose their phenomenally well-honed taste-buds to as many sublime and challenging epicurean experiences as they are able and be uncompromising about treating each and every mealtime as a special occasion worthy of the best ingredients. But the supra Foodie scholar will voraciously pursue greater culinary knowledge through exacting alpha culinary classes (at best more akin to professional stages) and ultra-specialist Foodie tours, offering fertile opportunity for intellectual foraging with esteemed Foodie heroes and fellow Foodiephiles.

IF THEIR IMMEDIATE SOCIAL CIRCLE IS NOT SUFFICIENTLY FOODIE, they may join one of the growing number of supper clubs. These are the co-ed equivalent of San Sebastian's sociedad gastronomica, where the like-palated show off their culinary skills, explain their dishes and share their knowledge and gustatory experiences with fellow Foodies. A Better Foodie book club also entices. Each Better Foodie prepares a different dish from a chosen new or seminal culinary bible and talks their fellow foodiephiles through its preferably obscure or extremely seasonal, hard-to-track-down ingredients and techniques – with a good helping of post-dinner Foodie discussion, too.

ENLIGHTENED CHEFS, such as arch-Foodie Jeremy Lee at London's Blueprint Café (and more are bound to follow), have set up Better Foodie book evenings where a chosen Foodie icon talks about their culinary philosophy and experiences – and prepares an exemplary dinner.

FRENCH BETTER FOODIES WILL HAVE UNDOUBTEDLY ALREADY JOINED 'LE FOODING', which began as a rebellion against la grande cuisine and is now a genuine culinary movement. It has a deeply Better Foodie philosophy of fusing food and feeling, and currently runs events in Paris, introducing hip emerging chefs (as likely to cook terroir with integrity – cuisines grandmère – as break new culinary ground) to appreciative gastrocenti. Each year it holds a series of Grand Fooding d'Eté events – picnics hosted by top chefs including Michel Troisgros and Pierre Herme.

ALL BETTER FOODIES ARE WHOLLY ENAMOURED with markets, so cookery courses at fabled markets make terribly good sense. Among the best are those held at La Boqueria in Barcelona, The Ferry Building Market in San Francisco and The Queen Victoria market in Melbourne.

Always in pursuit of greater gustatory knowledge...

...Better Foodies seek out specialist food museums and may even organise the gastro equivalent of a Grand Tour – after all food and culture are inextricably linked. The European Grand Gastro Tour should include: The National Museum of Pasta in Rome, collected by the Agnelli family; Munich's Potato Museum, The Museum of Bread in Paris, Auguste Escoffier at Villeneuve-Lambert on the Côte d'Azur and The Museum of Mustard in Dijon. A world tour would encompass The New York Museum of Food (including a pickle wing!), Seoul's Museum of Kimchi, Tokyo's Ramen Museum (complete with a number of noodle shops for sampling varieties) and St Petersburg's Bread Museum.

CLUBS FOR EVERY BETTER FOODIE CULINARY CRAVING ARE ALREADY THRIVING IN NEW YORK: 'Culinary Insiders' gives restaurant-obsessed gastronomes otherwise off-menu opportunities to attend dinners and gastro-tours hosted by seminal chefs and 'foodie' is the dinner equivalent of a rave, held in rented loft spaces around the city. There are rumoured to be more elite clandestine occasional supper clubs of Better Foodies in Paris, Berlin and London, too, but why wait around to be invited…inaugurate your own.

THOUGH ONLY PROFESSIONAL FOOD WRITERS MAY JOIN THE GUILD OF FOOD WRITERS and its international equivalents, Better Foodies may cultivate the friendship of a member and hope to be invited to one of their esoteric monthly workshops on specialist Better Foodie subjects – from artisanal and whey butters to the resurgence of mutton.

COMMITTED FOODIES PONDER ENROLLING ON AN MA IN GASTRONOMY at The University of Adelaide's Research Centre for the History of Food & Drink, in association with Le Cordon Bleu International (on-line students accepted), or Thames Valley University's BSc in International Culinary Arts whose alumni include Michelin-starred, molecularly-inclined chef John Campbell of The Vineyard.

RAISING THE GASTRO-GAME BY DEEPLY CONNECTING WITH THE INGREDIENT IN ITS HOME TERROIR rather than merely cooking in gorgeous surroundings is the natural extension of the cookery course for the Better Foodie. We yearn for active, intrepid gourmet adventure: deep-sea tuna fishing in Sicily, collecting bush ingredients for Maori cooking on a Navigator tour of Auckland or hands-on participation in a cocoa plantation in Venezuela.

THE MOST FIXATED, CEREBRAL BETTER FOODIE longingly peruses the prospectus of the University of Gastronomic Science founded by Slow Food and based at a restored Savoy estate in Piedmont, Italy, where food is elevated to an academic subject. Taught by gastronomic luminaries from around the world, courses (including a two year post-graduate degree) embrace all manner of sensory evaluation and chef-style 'stages', with artisan food producers. Tempting, too, is Slow Food's Master of Food (on-line studying possible) covering eighteen subjects (inevitably with an Italian bias) as diverse as cheese, animal breeds, balsamic vinegar, bread, pasta, the culture and history of gastronomy in literature, food science and semiotics.

UNSURPRISINGLY, MANY BETTER FOODIES SECRETLY ASPIRE TO BECOMING FOOD WRITERS, joining the waiting list for London's City University's evening courses run by food writing guru Lulu Grimes. Highly respected US writer David Leite runs occasional courses in New York for mediabistro.com in SoHo. Gotham Writers' Workshop offers classes for food enthusiasts with a penchant for food writing in New York, too. Simmering epi-culinary creativity is nurtured by The Writing Salon in Berkeley, California. University of British Columbia in Vancouver runs food-writing courses, including an annual gastro-immersion in Languedoc with ample opportunity for devouring and being inspired by local delicacies. The University of Adelaide dishes up occasional food writing courses balancing the tough reality with the redoubtable pleasure of eating exceptionally well.

THE BETTER FOODIE SCHOLAR will probably eschew (or have moved on from) the hedonistic Tuscan cookery school experience in favour of more esoteric specialist courses. Of course, the once yearly courses taught by Giulano Hazan (son of hallowed Marcella) at Villa San Michele are an exception to somewhat gastro-snobby attitudes to Italian cooking holidays.

THE TRULY ACADEMIC WILL WANT TO EXPERIENCE THE ANNUAL OXFORD SYMPOSIUM ON FOOD AND COOKERY, founded by the esteemed Alan Davidson, the author of the definitive Foodie bible, *The Oxford Campanion to Food*. This is a gathering of the top echelons of the most Foodie-minded writers and scholars – from *Saveur* editor Colman Andrews to Elizabeth Luard and Claudia Roden. Each year symposiasts debate issues ranging from authenticity to eggs, cutting across difficult and deliciously provocative intellectual Foodie terrain and create appropriate feasts to edibly illustrate their views. An additional annual food history and traditions symposium is held in the Spring in York, serving up equally esoteric debate. A recent focus was moulded foods (from Tudor quiddony to the present) and mould-makers including trailblazing Victorian writer, Mrs Marshall, who pre-empted (and inspired) Heston Blumenthal's liquid nitrogen and ice-cream experiments.

BETTER FOODIES AVIDLY CONSUME GASTRO-HISTORY BOOKS. Biographies of Escoffier, Carême, Soyer et al lie nonchalantly on the coffee table beside the sweetmeats (elvas plums, muscatel raisins still on the stalk, proper Hazer Baba Turkish delight) and impress fellow Foodie guests. Extremely erudite Better Foodies know about Ivan Day, a distinguished culinary historian with a passion for re-creating period dishes. They're already contemplating a course at his seventeenth-century farmhouse on the edge of the Lake District on roasting meats on an open fire (such as hogget with oysters), or hands-on workshops on moulded desserts and ices.

THEY RELISH THE IDEA OF ORGANISING A TAILORMADE seafood or game cookery workshop with a group of suitably food savvy friends at a luxurious retreat with a state-of-the-art kitchen such as Myer's Castle at Auchtermuchty.

WHAT THE CONSUMMATE FOODIE REALLY LUSTS AFTER is bespoke, one-on-one masterclass 'internment' in an elite Michelin kitchen; a few days of experiencing the sharp end of current culinary chemistry, with all the latest culinary gadgets and a batterie of palate-redefining techniques, from low temperature meat cooking to terrine making and espuma creation with John Campbell of The Vineyard.

HAVING ACQUIRED A TASTE FOR CULINARY FULFLMENT, the Better Foodie may try to extend it to their workplace, instigating culinary alternatives to the more usual corporate bonding exercises.

BETTER FOODIES ARE NOT ENTHRALLED BY CELEBRITY CHEF COURSES and would rather have the kudos of working in a Michelin-starred kitchen – especially if, as at Raymond Blanc's Le Manoir Aux Quat Saisons, it offers behind-the-scenes insight into the kitchen brigade in action – it's the culinary equivalent of front row tickets at a grand slam. Of course, they seek out the more unusual: patisserie in Eric Chavot's two Michelin star Capital Hotel in London, which skips the basics, immediately progressing to making Pierre Hermé/Peychard style macaroons and serious chocolate tempering and ganache making; the truly committed may inveigle their way onto a course at Valrhona's HQ near Lyon. Other ultra-Foodie courses include Malaysian-Australian Tony Tan's Asian cuisine and culinary tours in Melbourne, Asia and Spain; Patricia Wells, the venerable Herald Tribune food critic's shopping and cooking courses in Paris and Provence and wild herb aficionado Simon Rogan's Cumbrian workshops including insight into the latest cheffy gadgets and techniques.

Serial supra Foodies will seek alpha cookery classes...

...around the world to perfect their culinary finesse and master the more challenging techniques. Cutting edge knife skills, fish filleting, breadmaking, butchery (courses with Marylebone's much-admired Ginger Pig which evolve into dinner with the demonstrated cut at La Fromagerie are deeply Better Foodie) are especially sought after. The uncompromising Better Foodie enrols at schools with the stature of Leiths in London, The French Culinary Institute in New York, The Ritz Escoffier, Alain Ducasse's professional culinary school/thinktank in Paris, or the exacting professional standards of Billingsgate Seafood Cookery School.

My Better Foodie heroes
stellar culinary figures who've immeasurably influenced my Better Foodie calling

Better Foodies are an idiosyncratic, greedily opinionated bunch. There are certain names that any self-respecting Better Foodie refers to with suitable awe and affection, and would relish the opportunity to share a table with. This is, necessarily, a very personal perspective (and absolutely not in any particular order of ranking); a batterie of those whom I especially respect, who make me think about food in fresh and different ways or whose dishes I find irresistible, often thrillingly challenging and who've (sometimes unwittingly) helped make me a better and more committed Foodie.

John Campbell Destined for the highest gastro-heights and tipped for two-Michelin status in the near future, his kitchen epitomises the calm, organised kitchen we should all – professional and home high Foodies alike – aspire to. Often dubbed the 'celebral' chef, not only does he practise the better elements of molecular gastronomy, but has patiently explained many of its intricacies to a chemistry-phobic Foodie (me).

Raymond Blanc Indefatigably passionate, not to mention eminently quotable on everything from organics and growing Asian vegetables in the UK to the most sensual food. His very workable *Cooking for Friends* book was my first high Foodie cookbook, which I continue to use avidly.

Alice Waters Unabashedly a culinary heroine of mine for being far, far in the vanguard of extolling the virtues of the best tasting and most humanely raised/grown produce. I greatly admire her, admittedly utopian, vision of culinary classrooms, too, and was thrilled to meet her and experience her divine food at Le Manoir Aux Quat Saison's American Revolution Festival – a truly historic Better Foodie occasion.

Monica Lavery Introduced the delights of authentic chorizo, smoked pimenton, Ortiz anchovies/tuna and the extreme pleasure of pata negra acorn-fed Iberico ham and many more Spanish delicacies to devoted Foodies, who rapidly graduated from Brindisa's trademark Borough Market's chorizo and rocket roll to creating their own Hispanic feasts.

Giorgio Locatelli His pasta transcends any other and his impassioned and utterly genuine welcome of Better Foodie-in-the-making children to his supra-glamorous Locanda Locatelli is truly heart-warming (my son rates his grissini, risotto and ice-cream as the best ever.)

Michel Roux, Senior Apart from having arguably the sexiest accent in British gastronomy (I confess I once kept a message from him on my answerphone for weeks!), his soufflés are incomparable and he probably has the world's finest gastro-address book. On a once-in-a-lifetime commission to cover the annual Roux Scholarship for young chefs with Michel Roux in Spain, I'll never forget arriving in Barcelona at close to midnight, after a Bilbao to London flight had been cancelled. Michel dismissed the airport hotel dining room, phoned a friend, and we were whisked off to an intoxicatingly frenetic tapas bar/restaurant for probably the best midnight feast I'm ever likely to experience.

Gerard Coleman Creates the most exquisite chocolates in the UK, including the salted caramels served at Gordon Ramsay at Claridges and the Better Foodie riposte to the After Eight chocolate: Moroccan Mint discs of refined, delicate sophistication. His workshops are a must for all Better Foodies wanting to understand chocolate more deeply.

Henrietta Green Her *Food Lover's Guide to Britain* first brought UK artisan producers to the attention of Better Foodies-in-the-making. An incredibly detailed, thorough and witty work, which I only wish she might update – although it would probably run to several volumes now.

Ferran Adria So iconic his name has entered Foodie lexicon: Adria-ism is equated with avant-garde, multi-sensory, multi-course eating. He is refreshingly open to sharing his latest discoveries – some, admittedly, on the edge of edibility. In high Foodie circles he's also known for giving in-depth workshops – though it's less highly publicised that he and his brother, Albert (who masterminds desserts at El Bulli and runs their Barcelona lab) are brilliant dancers – as witnessed at a Lavazza party at Salone del Gusto!

Heston Blumenthal

Arguably now the most famous British chef for
his highly inquisitive, laced with liberal humour,
audacious approach to bringing chemistry into the
kitchen. Despite his fame he remains a great, self-
deprecating, down-to-earth chef (whose classical
dishes are brilliant, too). He still has plenty of time
for talking to food writers like myself.

'*It is a hard matter, my fellow citizens, to argue with the belly, since it has no ears.*'

Mestrius Plutarch, Greek historian, biographer and philosopher.

Fay Maschler Undisputed doyenne of restaurant criticism in London, whose opinions even the most cynical Better Foodie, convinced of their own stellar palate, can't help but respect and be guided by.

Elizabeth David No Better Foodie can fail to be riveted by her imperious, yet utterly refreshing, culinary style, even though it is now difficult to appreciate quite how shockingly different her vivid descriptions of food in France, Italy, Greece and North Africa were in 1960.

Ruth Reichl Reading and revelling in her autobiography, *Comfort Me With Apples*, she subconsciously fed into my psyche and influenced the planning of this book… and because she's probably got the ultimate arch-Foodie's job: editor-in-chief of US magazine, *Gourmet*.

Jill Norman Ushered Elizabeth David, Jane Grigson and Alan Davidson into the culinary consciousness of post-war Britain as their publisher at Penguin – and is a highly-erudite, much-travelled food writer herself. (On meeting her recently, I was thrilled that she acknowledged the time was ripe for poking gentle fun at those of us who are sometimes too intently serious about their food.)

Nigella Lawson Wonderfully personal, greedy, evocative prose…and I share her Foodie passions for anchovies and chestnuts.

James Beard Prolific food writer, teacher and promoter of good food, he played a pivotal role in the changing dining habits of America and tirelessly encouraged an appreciation of its own cuisine. His former home in New York is now The James Beard Foundation and workshops and dinners take place in his former kitchen (high on my priority list of places to visit).

Tim and Nina Zagat Possessing an awe-inspiring and prodigious appetite, Tim claims to often 'do' five restaurants a day. His menu memory is legendary, and needs to be, as he's founder/publisher of Zagat guides, alongside his equally culinarily-charged wife Nina. Sharing lunch with Tim Zagat at Jean-Georges in New York, experiencing the respect he inspires and his 'working the room' technique, was truly edifying.

Alan Davidson A former diplomat-turned-academic high Foodie writer, the late Alan Davidson compiled *The Oxford Companion to Food* – the bible for every Better Foodie who wants detailed, historic and erudite explanations of essential and arcane edible-related information.

Peter Gordon With seemingly inexhaustible sources of wonderful and recondite ingredients to thrill the most restless Foodie, he is always enormously kind and fun, and captured on film for posterity my lushest high Foodie assignment to Dom Perignon; a veritable high Foodie 'last supper' where Peter Gordon, alongside chefs Angela Hartnett, David Thompson, John Campbell and Andre Garrett indulged in their most daring dishes to match with vintage champagnes for the delectation of Dom Perignon's chef de cave and myself!

Anna del Conte Not only is her opus, *Gastronomy of Italy*, the most delightful reference for gastro Italophiles, her lemon pasta the most effective almost-believe-it's-summer simple culinary pick-me-up, but her melodic voice talking food is very soothing.

Patricia Michelson For her unerring passion and infinite knowledge of the finest cheeses and her impeccable taste, which makes La Fromagerie one of the most wonderful and dangerous places to wallow in.

Stephanie Alexander

A seminal force in championing Australian cooking
and ingredients, her arch-Better Foodie philosophy
is to encourage would-be Foodies to try unfamiliar
ingredients, seek out specialist producers and
preferably visit them at source.

What does 'mantecare' mean in a recipe?

Add butter towards the end of cooking (as when cooking risotto).

What is the difference between aïoli and aïllade?

Aïoli is a garlic mayonnaise traditionally served with fish bourride; aïllade, also from Provence, has walnuts and grainy mustard, too, and is usually spread on crostini or used as an accompaniment to more robust fish.

What is zampone, often eaten at Italian New Year celebrations, better known as?

Pig's trotter.

Is vegetables à la greque served warm or cold?

Cold. It is a mix of violet artichokes, button onions, mushrooms and cauliflower cooked with lots of herbs (thyme, garlic, coriander seeds and saffron), with tomato and basil added towards the end.

What British winter vegetable is silver beet better known as (it also comes in a ruby version)?

Chard.

What is a kaiten sushi restaurant?

Conveyor belt sushi.

What is agar-agar?

An extract of seaweed, which is made into translucent crumpled strips and is the more cheffy and vegetarian alternative to gelatine, preferred for its setting. It comes from the Indian/Pacific ocean.

Is it a good sign if a mature Gruyère weeps?

This is only the salt melting through the cheese. It suggests it has been carefullly produced and will, therefore, have a good, grainy, nutty, fruity taste.

Why is a pacojet the most longed for piece of kitchen gadgetry among many aspiring chefs?

It makes instant ices.

Who first gave the cranberry its name and why?

Pilgrim Fathers thinking its blossom resembled the head of a crane.

THE BETTER FOODIE
FOODIE
almanac

Seasonal almanac
an insider's guide to embracing quintessential gastro-seasonal ingredients and festivals

The Better Foodie's calendar is liberally and discerningly peppered with their very own scrupulously seasonal sagras; timely reminders to be on full alert for the first-of-the-season purple sprouting broccoli, samphire or quince – in Better Foodie circles, it's reason enough to celebrate with a festive meal dedicated to the revered ingredient. Better still, the Better Foodie revels in discovering and making pilgrimages to gastro-festivals, whether highly obscure – the Saffron Fair in Consuegra near Toledo in Spain each last weekend in October – or deeply gastronomical gatherings of top echelon culinary heroes.

IT'S TANTAMOUNT TO A BETTER FOODIE MANIFESTO: the simple pleasure of eating seasonally makes food taste inexorably so much better and adds gustatory spice to life. The Better Foodie never suffers from seasonal disorder as there's invariably something sublimely scrumptious to get excited about. Of course, every self-respecting Better Foodie with integrity subscribes to the local and seasonal mantra, but their sybaritic gastro-radar also extends beyond. And when the season for each greatly anticipated comestible is over, absence only makes the heart grow fonder…

THE BETTER FOODIE IS, ALSO, MORE THAN USUALLY PRONE TO INCURABLE SYMPTOMS OF FOODIE FESTIVITIES – treating the world as a grazing menu offering endless tantalising opportunities to dip into food fests, as a perfect justification for a year-round diet of gastro-breaks. Some pilgrimages are non-negotiable – every passionate Better Foodie must visit Slow Food's Salone del Gusto at least once in their life – while others should be treated more opportunistically. I confess to the odd wild goose chase when makeshift fly-posting has lured me down endless twisting country lanes to find several stalls of dubious provenance and a bunch of scowling locals in the depths of Tuscany. Many more food festivals turn out be charming manifestations of arcane, specialist parochialism. At best there's opportunity for much sniffing, tasting, buying and discussing among like-minded devoted Better Foodies.

OF COURSE, SOME FESTIVALS, HOWEVER FOODIE, ARE MOSTLY CELEBRATED IN THE HOME. Undeterred, the ultra-determined Better Foodie abroad goes into full-on gastro-charm offensive – asking all the right epicurious questions at market – and triumphantly inveigles a coveted invite into the home of the suitably flattered Foodie who characteristically revels in sharing their culinary largesse.

January

FESTIVALS

NORTHCOTE MANOR FOOD & WINE FESTIVAL, UK Attracts chefs of peak international calibre (Heston Blumenthal of The Fat Duck and Andoni Luis Aduriz of San Sebastian's Mugaritz were recent stars) to strut their gastro-credentials in a week of formidable dinners alongside resident chef, Nigel Haworth, at one of northwest England's finest country hotels.

WINTER RESTAURANT WEEK Canny Better Foodie gastro-travellers visit New York at the end of January for this treat. Several upscale dining establishments offer special menus at prices too tempting to ignore. Similar deals take place in San Francisco, Washington DC, Vancouver and London.

LA GRAN FESTA DE LA CALÇOTADA, CATALONIA On the last Sunday in January. Celebrating the new season for a variety of exceptionally long spring onions: char-grilled in vast quantities on an open fire and eaten dipped in romesco sauce.

MADRID FUSION An electrifying gathering of international avant garde chefs who discuss and demonstrate the latest culinary techniques and discoveries – an opportunity for Better Foodies to rub shoulders with top international food writers, too.

UP HELLY AA CELEBRATIONS, SHETLAND ISLANDS, UK A torch-lit ritual burning of a Viking longship and a ceilidh, with reestit mutton (cured and dried by hanging over an open peat fire) and bannocks.

Seville or bitter oranges Burnt ember in colour, and not only for the homemade marmalade every Better Foodie proudly proffers on their breakfast table, but also for making outrageously good orange curd, piquant salad dressing with walnut oil and mustard and to add fragrant zest to soups, stews – even mayonnaise. Candied, they're the best rind to dip into proper chocolate.

Sicilian blood oranges Better Foodies adore these for their flavour and aesthetic drama. The most sought after are the completely seedless Tarocco. They make fetching salads, especially with slivers of roast aubergine and a liberal sprinkling of fresh pomegranate seeds. The juice is head-turning with prosecco as an aperitif.

Italian cime di rapa (or friar's beard) It's high season for these sprouting tender chive-like greens related to, and tasting reminiscent of, turnip, with a bitter, peppery edge. Cook quickly like spinach and serve as part of an antipasti verdura or as a stuffing with buffalo ricotta in homemade ravioli.

Dried chickpeas from Liguria Knowing Better Foodies snap up these new season specimens, which are more tender, so need less cooking than older pulses. Use for making all manner of soups and salads with a Southern Italian or Middle Eastern edge.

February

Violetta di chioggi Purple leafed artichoke from Northern Italy eaten whole, sliced thinly in a salad or deep-fried and rolled in polenta – for antipasto di verdura. Better Foodies bottle their own, selecting only the smallest, tightest buds to infuse with lemon, marjoram and bayleaf in extra virgin olive oil.

Fresh lotus flower root Has an intriguing lacey texture and mildly sweet interior and is auspicious eaten at Chinese New Year celebrations, as it is said that good luck passes through the holes of the lotus root and into the mouth for the year to come – and it adds a subtle crunch to adventurous salads and stir-fries.

Luscious Israeli persimmons At their best to satisfy February tropical fruit cravings, as are luscious South African Cape grapes – particularly the crisp-textured La Rochelle variety.

FESTIVALS

SAN FRANCISCO CRAB FESTIVAL, US Celebrates the incomparably succulent Dungeness crab that has been fished off the Californian coast since 1840. Devour stuffed, baked, sautéed or, best of all, steamed straight off the boat, matched with local sourdough and Chardonnay. There are also plenty of crab-centric events and crab dishes on menus throughout the neighbourhood. (www.sfvisitor.org/crab)

LEMON FESTIVAL IN MENTON On the French Riveria. Parades and citrus sculptures, besides tastings and alluring lemon-centric menus. (villedementon.com)

LUNAR NEW YEAR/SPRING FESTIVAL IN SHANGHAI AND CHINATOWNS EVERYWHERE Spectacular, exhilarating and often chaotic with dragon and lion dances, fireworks and much feasting on jiaozi dumplings and niango (a sticky rice cake).

VIOLET FESTIVAL IN TOULOUSE, SOUTHWEST FRANCE Scores highly among Better Foodies for gathering inspiration for recherché menus. Sample violet syrups, jams, mustard, foie gras, vinegars and chocolate from artisan producers, and violet-themed restaurant menus.

SOUTH BEACH MIAMI FOOD FESTIVAL, US Attracts stellar chefs of Ferran Adria status, making it a magnet for sun-seeking Better Foodies with its backdrop of the Atlantic American Riveria. With tastings of signature dishes of the most noteworthy local restaurants.

March

Fresh, new season garlic With a subtle sweet pungency. The leaves are good in salads, too. Sample tiny white-flowered wild garlic – also known as ransoms or ramps – and Fiddlehead ferns (young fern fronds picked before they unfurl), which resemble the scroll at the top of a fiddle – rarely found outside the US, they make for a recherché garnish sautéed in butter.

Sea kale shoots Creamy white with the merest purple tinge. Delectable served Sardinian style with lemon and bottarga.

The first flush single estate early Darjeeling The Better Foodie tea connoisseur eagerly anticipates these tender young leaf shoots – though their exact timing is wholly dependent on the winter rains. An arch delicacy, the tea – always drunk without milk – has a fresh aroma and almost muscatel flavour.

FESTIVALS

BLACK PUDDING FAIR, MONTAGNE-AU-PERCHE, NORMANDY, FRANCE
Definitely not for fainthearted Better Foodies, this is three days of artisan butchers and boudin noir aficionados revelling in all manner of black pudding exploits and culinary combinations. (normandy-tourism.org)

MASLENITSA FESTIVAL, MOSCOW, RUSSIA
A blini and firework celebration of Spring.

CIOCCOLATO, TURIN, ITALY
A must for chocophiles, with stalls vaunting favourite Better Foodie chocolatiers including: Amadei, Gobino and Domori. Also, interactive exhibits recreating a cacao plantation and all aspects of production, chocolate-themed dinners, and chocolate-related literary readings and performances at exquisite nineteenth-century cafés.

MELBOURNE FOOD AND WINE FESTIVAL, VICTORIA, AUSTRALIA
What Better Foodie could resist the prospect of participating in The World's Longest Lunch, purloining culinary inspiration from ultra-creative visiting chefs (Teague Ezard and Peter Gordon are regulars) and eating their way around Melbourne's melting pot of Vietnamese, Spanish and singularly Australian cuisine.

HANAMI IN JAPAN
The annual cherry blossom viewing ritual. The Better Foodie goes prepared, purchasing an elaborate lacquered bento box of onigiri, (fish, pickled plum and rice) to feast on to prevent melancholy descending as the blossom falls to the ground.

April

Bassano white asparagus from Veneto Prized as a fleetingly available arch delicacy by asparagus aficionados – especially as it precedes the asparagus season proper. It is exceptionally plump, yet tender, and is traditionally eaten garnished with chopped boiled egg.

White polenta A cherished Slow Food Presidia product from Fruili-Venezia Giulia in Italy. This freshly ground new season polenta made from mais biancaperla – stunning with delicate cuttlefish and ink sauce.

FESTIVALS

BAYONNE HAM FAIR, FRANCE Most Better Foodies take their charcuterie connoisseurship very seriously and believe the delicious salt cured ham of Bayonne (a Basque outpost of southwest France) deserves due recognition – alongside its prosciutto and serrano rivals – and relish indulging in frenzied terroir feasting. (www.ville-bayonne.fr)

SNAIL FÊTE, OSENBACH, ALSACE, FRANCE For the Better Foodie curious to explore the snail beyond garlic butter. Experience all manner of Alsacian snail dishes and bet on a traditional snail tierce on a specially designed racetrack.

SCOTTSDALE CULINARY FESTIVAL IN ARIZONA, US Native American, Latin and contemporary US chefs converge in a week-long, taste-bud challenging series of events. (www.scottsdaleculinaryfestival.org)

ARTICHOKE FESTIVAL, PAESTUM, CAMPANIA, ITALY Feast on Tondi di Paestum (rounded, thornless, pink-hued artichokes) fried, roasted, baked, on pasta, pizza, in frittatas and more.

SONGKRAN (THAI NEW YEAR), BANGKOK, THAILAND Aside from water-throwing mayhem (to encourage good rains for the harvest) street food hawkers are out in force: graze on pad thai noodles; krayasad puffed rice with oats, peanuts and Thai noodles, sweetened with palm sugar and coconut syrup; kanom tom sticky rice and mung bean balls. Fortunate Better Foodies chance on khao chae: a special rice dish cooked in jasmine blossom water.

May

FESTIVALS

LA LOUCHE D'OR IN LILLE, FRANCE Chefs converge from all over the world to slurp and celebrate soup at the so-called golden ladle festival.

SAGRA DEL PESCE, CAMOGLI, LIGURIA, ITALY A huge fry-up of local fish in three-metre-wide pans all along the waterfront of the sleepy cobbled village of Camogli on the Ligurian Riviera, close to Genoa.

NINTH AVENUE FOOD FESTIVAL, NEW YORK, US Masses of stalls line 37th – 57th Street selling every conceivable delicacy and speciality. Neighbourhood stores and restaurants pull out the epicurean stops, too.

CAPE GOURMET FESTIVAL, SOUTH AFRICA Stellar international chef demo line-up, taste workshops – including potjiekos: food slow-cooked in a cast-iron, three-legged pot over charcoal – and a picnic from the artisan producer market on Table Mountain. (www.gourmetsa.com)

Hopshoots, known as bruscandoli From Venice, where they have long been considered the Spring recherché vegetable for risotto. They make a delicious and pleasingly rarefied alternative to wild asparagus, with a hint of almonds and artichoke and a spicy aftertaste.

Jersey Royals Distinguished by their papery skins and distinctive creamy, almost hazelnut flavour, they supersede every other luxury potato for sheer gustatory pleasure.

Charentais melon Highly scented and vividly orange. Delectable served with Gascon floc (grape must and Armagnac).

Alphonso mango from India Orange-yellow with a mouth-watering, seductive perfume and exquisite melting silken flesh, with hints of peach, pineapple, pear and lychee. Best eaten messily. This is the absolute antithesis of year-round good-looking, never ripe, insipid (picked when immature) fibrous supermarket mango.

Asian loquats Small orange, pear-shaped fruit – tastes somewhere between a melon and a papaya with lime astringency. Good roasted with orange blosom honey and used in many Sichuan recipes.

June

Samphire Delicate, aromatic, salty and similar to wild asparagus. Preferably hand-picked by Better Foodies on a fervently Foodie Norfolk or San Francisco Bay outing. Lightly cooked and dressed with extra-virgin olive oil and lemon it elevates every fish dish.

Baby beetroot To roast for a salad. Better Foodie parents use this to colour icing for cupcakes – for those all-important school fête cake stalls.

Cherries Better Foodies appreciate the huge variety – from almost white to ruby red – for clafoutis, ices and preserves. We especially savour the deep, slightly sour flavour of Morello.

Fraises des bois Wild strawberries intense, exquisite berry flavour. Too fragile to travel, so are ideally eaten straight from the market stall in Monaco for an impromptu picnic – the Better Foodie epitome of summer.

Pakistani mangoes Larger, thinner, more curvy and sweeter. Most popular are Sindi, Langra and Chaunsa.

Wild salmon From Scotland or Alaska – with an incomparable delicacy and finesse.

FESTIVALS

MANGO FESTIVAL IN DELHI, INDIA Talkatora Gardens showcases awesome mango exhibits, tastings and eating competitions.

TASTE OF GRAMPIAN, INVERURIE, ABERDEENSHIRE, UK
A one day event championing regional produce and chefs.

GOUTATOU IN ARBOIS, FRANCHE-COMTÉ, FRANCE Maturing well and likely to become one of the biggest food festivals in France, with plentiful opportunity for tasting regional delicacies including Morteau and Comté, plus workshops and a communal banquet.

TASTE OF LONDON, UK Sheer epicurean pleasure for savvy Better Foodies who pride themselves on knowing their restaurants. Stellar chefs from more than 40 restaurants offer samples of their dishes, including iconic, hard-to-book Le Gavroche, The Connaught and Pied à Terre, plus specialist food producers, taste workshops and hands-on cookery classes.

PEMBROKESHIRE FISH WEEK, UK Includes seafood tapas tasting, rockpool rambles, learn-to-fish workshops, fishy tales and tastings for children, crab lunches, seafood barbecues and fish masterclasses.

HOMAGE TO KUGELHOPF IN RIBEAUVILLE, ALSACE, FRANCE
Yeast-enriched dome-shaped cake that is taken very seriously by Alsace Better Foodies.

July

Borlotti beans Fresh, creamy, nutty and striated with deep pinky-red flecks (Better Foodies hardly need reminding not to cook them in salted water otherwise they'll be tough – and only season just before serving).

Zucchini (courgette) flowers For frying in a light batter or stuffing with lemon-ricotta or mozzarella, breadcrumbs, anchovy and parsley.

Flat peaches or saturna Small and flat with an almondy perfume; hugely popular in Gascony. Also rare Italian white nectarines.

Gooseberries Quintessentially English: pale yellowish, floral fragrant and sweet enough to eat raw; greener examples require cooking and puréeing to accompany barbecued mackerel or the most summery of fools.

FESTIVALS

LE MARCHÉ AUX FRUITS ROUGES, NOYON, NORTHERN FRANCE

Farmers gather outside the cathedral to sell not only the red fruits (cherries, currants and raspberries) but their jams, compotes, syrups and beers, wondrous tarts, ice-creams and Le Coeur de Noyon bonbons.

SHEDIAC LOBSTER FESTIVAL, NEW BRUNSWICK, US

Lobster roll and whole boiled lobster feasting. Also a lobster eating contest: participants must eat the meat of three whole lobsters in three minutes using no tools: a mean feat even for the highly trained Better Foodie.

SINGAPORE FOOD FESTIVAL

A month-long celebration of Singapore's exhilaratingly diverse food culture: a Tok Panjang banquet, workshops including Chinese tea-tasting on an Island cruise, Malay, Indian and Chinese Rojak, and a festive food taste trail in Chinatown (fruit, vegetables and shrimp salads with fried dough fritters).

REDENTORE FESTIVAL, VENICE, ITALY

On the third weekend in July. In 1576 the city was struck by a plague and the desperate Venetians made a deal with God, promising to build a temple on Giudecca island where they would give thanks every July if they were saved. Each year the spectacular procession to the island crosses a 'boat-bridge' of gondolas moored end-to-end across the lagoon. After spectacular fireworks, feasting begins in earnest. Better Foodies should try to wrangle an invite to an extravagant Venetian picnic, or make their own.

August

FESTIVALS

CHILLI FIESTA AT WEST DEAN GARDENS, WEST SUSSEX, UK
The culinary event for heat-seekers, showing over 250 chilli varieties and all manner of chilli comestibles for the adventurous chilli fanatic. www.westdean.org.uk

GARLIC FESTIVAL, ISLE OF WIGHT, UK
Alliumophiles stock up on chutneys, pickles, ice cream and fudge, besides attending workshops and garlic suffused menus. (www.garlicfestival.co.uk)

LAUTREC PINK GARLIC FESTIVAL, MIDI-PYRÉNÉES, FRANCE
A decidedly pungent affair: a huge garlic soup is prepared for communal feasting and competitions are held for the best pink garlic sculpture. Try the pink garlic tart. www.ailrosedelautrec.com

THE ARBROATH SEA FESTIVAL, UK
Celebrating Arbroath smokies (local haddock smoked over wood in an outdoor pit) on the beautiful harbourside in Arbroath.

EEL FESTIVAL IN ÅHUS MARKET SQUARE, SOUTHERN SWEDEN
Celebrate eels in every guise – pickled, fried, steamed and baked.

CRAWFISH AND FERMENTED HERRING FESTIVALS THROUGHOUT SWEDEN
At the end of August. These invariably involve much drinking of schnapps and eating Västerbotten cheese.

Chanterelles or girolles Better Foodies who happen on a woodland glut when foraging should savour these simply sautéed on bruschetta, or as a delicate accompaniment to scallops.

Hon-Shimeji A newly-fashionable cultivated Japanese mushroom, which grows in clusters and has a mildly sweet, almond flavour.

Cannellini beans Ivory white, fresh and creamy, these merit a trip to an Italian market, as their incomparable velvety texture make sublime salads – a totally different experience to even the better class of canned beans for the epicurious Better Foodie.

Mirabelles Precociously rare, succulent, small golden yellow plums from Lorraine, in northeastern France, which make sublime tarts. Better Foodies who alight on a trove of mirabelles feel it's only right to make a preserve to enjoy their tart yet honeyed flavour for longer.

English cobnuts Crisp, yet milky, juicy and suitably recherché in salads or roasted and crushed as cobnut meringue. Rare enough to keep many a Better Foodie guessing. For a moreish seasonal snack let guests crack their own and dip juicy kernels in sea salt. Order from: www.cobnuts.co.uk.

Fresh tarbais beans From Tarbes, in the Hautes-Pyrénées. The only Label Rouge bean – hand-harvested, large white beans with a thin skin and subtle, rich flavour. Tarbais are an essential ingredient for cassoulet and garbure and are good in salads, too.

September

Fresh piquillo peppers From Navarra, Spain. These are hand-picked and sun-dried with intense flavour.

Cardoons Resembling giant bunches of thistle-spiked celery and rarely seen, as they are snapped up by Better Foodie connoisseurs for their tender inner stalks, which taste of a sweeter cross between artichoke and salsify. In Italy the most tender (de-stringed) stalks are eaten raw, dipped into Piedmontese warm anchovy bagna cauda. Mostly blanched and baked in a gratin or finished with a light sauce of egg yolk, lemon and parsley.

Damsons Dusty purple-black and too tart to eat raw, multi-talented damsons make for delectable pickle, rose-scented jam or sorbet. The knowing Better Foodie cooks a portion of their jam down further to make damson cheese, a decadent dessert preferably served with lashings of cream.

Turkish figs Luscious purple-black, scarlet-fleshed and aromatic. Sublime with best buffalo mozzarella, burrata or San Daniele ham in salads, or baked in rose petal or cardamom-scented honey syrup.

Festivals
The Great British Cheese Festival, Cheltenham, UK
More than 450 cheeses to taste and buy plus associated gourmet comestibles from British artisan producers, taste workshops in the School for Big Cheese, antiquarian cook books and cheese collectibles. (www.thecheeseweb.com)

Slow Food cheese festival, Bra, Italy Biennial with the next
in 2007. A mesmerising, blissful Better Foodie opportunity to taste and discuss cheeses with artisan producers worldwide.

World Oyster Eating Championship, Hillsborough,
IRELAND The International Oyster Festival. hillsboroughoysterfestival.com

Mussel festival at La Braderie, Lille, France A giant
moules fest/brocante market during the first weekend of September.

Moon Festival in China and Hong Kong Marks the end of
harvest season. Moon cake pastries, or uebing, are the most important symbol. They are filled with fruit, date paste, bitter egg or, in Shanghai, red bean paste. Feast at midnight on just harvested crispy fried yams with black peppercorns, lotus roots wrapped and fried in special dough, fried fish with peanuts, pork in honey and ginger sauce, and spring onion pancakes.

A Taste of Slow, Victoria, Australia. Showcases local 'Slow'
producers with markets, hands-on cooking classes, forums, 'slow tables' or communal meals, and seasonal Slow menus in restaurants.

October

White truffles Preferably from around Alba in Piedmont. Their sublime aroma makes every Better Foodie weak at the knees. Prohibitive prices mean that, for many, the heavenly scent has to suffice. Yet even a modestly liberal shaving transforms the simplest tagliolini or risotti.

Cepes An extravagance most Better Foodies will run to at least once in the new season. Most daydream of discovering a halcyon, bountiful stash on a country walk, but aren't too proud to splurge on buying enough for a seasonal feast.

Vacherin Mont D'Or Already at its richest and most runny, unctuous, resiny best long before the festive build-up. Produced both in Jura and Switzerland. Good wintry wishful-skiing sustenance. Bake and serve with skins-on charlotte potatoes, pain de campagne and morteau (a smoked meat sausage from Franche-Comte).

Calasparra rice Most discerning Better Foodies claim to be able to distinguish new season rice from Murcia.

Chestnuts Not just for Christmas. Roasting fresh chestnuts – preferably foraged in the wild chestnut groves of La Corrèze in the Limousin region of southwest France – is an autumnal pleasure for French Better Foodies. Chestnuts are also memorable in soups, salads and add verve to the simplest vegetable gratin. The Chestnut festival in Mourjou is where Foodies celebrate this Autumn treat with all manner of artisan-produced delicacies, plus processions, competitions, a village feast and interludes of music and dancing.

Festivals

Salone del Gusto, Turin, Italy The Slow Food biennial festival (the next is in 2006) I urge every Better Foodie to visit and marvel at least once – truly gastro-nirvana. Halls of artisan producers from every corner of the globe urge you (the language of delectable food makes up for linguistic inadequacies) to sample their local speciality, whether anchovies only caught in the tiny Italian port of Nola, Tibetan cheese, fragoline di Ribera (intensely fragrant wild strawberries from Sicily), Ligurian rose syrup, Gascon black pig ham or Three Counties Perry from the UK. Also, specialist workshops (sheep cheeses, chestnuts, honeys), demos from iconic chefs – Alice Waters is a regular – and exceptional dinners in restaurants throughout the area.

National Mole Fair at San Pedro Actopan, South of Mexico City Plenty of mole sauce of unsweetened chocolate, pepper and spices demos and tastes. www.andalemexico.com

Tasting Australia, Adelaide, Australia A biennial Southern Australian festival (the next is in 2007). Besides a headline international chef line-up, there are masterclasses, a feast of the spoken word with the world's best food writers, critics, academics and producers on subjects as diverse as gastro-porn v. kitchen classics; the future of cookbooks; and whether French cuisine is still haute.

Alba Truffle Festival, Piedmont, Italy In the central Piazza. Watch mesmerised as traders haggle over huge porcini and fist-sized truffles. With a market, plus a truffle auction attended by international top chefs.

November

FESTIVALS

WHITE TRUFFLE FESTIVAL ACQUALAGNA, LE MARCHE, ITALY

There is a market for spectating, inhaling and serious purchasing. Also, seminars and truffle-imbued restaurant menus.

ST MARTIN'S DAY, SWEDEN

Roast goose and black soup (made with goose blood) eaten to commemorate St. Martin of Tours and Martin Luther.

THE DAY OF THE DEAD IN OAXACA MEXICO, NOVEMBER 1ST

It's all about welcoming dead ancestors with a ritual meal including the 'Drink of the Gods' – chocolate atole (cocoa beans aged under earth, ground with wheat, rice and cinnamon, then kneaded, whisked and mixed with atole – a liquid made from boiling up corn dough – into a froth), tamales (spiced corn dough steamed in leaves and stuffed with pork), black bean purée with tiny balls of prized local quesillo cheese, crispy tostadas, anisey epazote leaves and turkey mole. Better Foodies not fortunate enough to be invited to a home in the build-up to the Day of the Dead can experience the fiesta-like atmosphere in Oaxaca markets with oil-drum braziers selling memelita (corn tortillas with lard), quesadillas, black beans cooked in clay pots, salsas and stuffed chillies to see you through the candlelit night.

HENRIETTA GREEN FOOD LOVERS FAIR IN COVENT GARDEN, LONDON, UK

Always a very discerning choice of key UK artisan producers and cookery demonstrations – and a chance to meet the author.

Puntarelle A favourite among Better Foodies wanting to offer competitively Foodie guests a satisfyingly recondite seasonal starter. It's a wild looking chicory-related green. The hollow inner hearts are cut into thin shreds and immersed in iced water to curl. Its bitter-sweet crispness is addictive. Serve as in Roman cuisine with a punchy anchovy vinaigrette.

Celeriac Deeply savoury for caper-piquant celeriac remoulade, with a properly raised Melton Mowbray pork pie, or Better Foodie roasted celeriac chips.

Pomegranates Ruby-red with glistening sweet-sour seeds within. Transform a saffron pilau, an aubergine salad or a Claudia Roden-inspired orange blossom winter salad. Or simply squeeze out the juice, as an orange, for a dressing or cocktail. Better Foodies proudly make their own pomegranate molasses, too.

Bitter-sweet wet walnuts Use them fresh in salads, breads or with pleasurably piquant blue cheese.

More recondite birds Aficionados are particularly partial to delicate, lightly hung Woodcock.

December

Malaga raisins from Andalucia Dusky plump and luscious, hand-harvested and sun-dried and usually sold in bunches on the vine. Perfect for the Better Foodie cheeseboard or in Malaga ice-cream, flan or warming, Moorish pork stews.

Radicchio di Treviso Bittersweet, pointy and brush-shaped, also known as trevise. Spectacular in salads or simply grilled.

Deglet Noor Luscious, almost fudge-like dates and larger, softer, succulent Medjool dates. Wrap with dry-cure bacon and grill; fragrant in a lamb tagine; for scones with a Middle Eastern twist; or stuff with homemade rosewater-scented marzipan as festive sweetmeats or Foodie gifts.

Percebes or gooseneck barnacles A rare seafood delicacy, almost exclusively from Galicia in northwest Spain. These are best tasted *in situ*, as only a few determined restaurateurs succeed in importing a precarious supply. Select unwrinkled, short fat percebes and cook by merely bringing them to a rolling boil and then drain. The Better Foodie adores their rarity and messy eating (napkin tied around the neck is de rigeur). To eat, first make an incision with your teeth in the long soft neck of the percebe, suck out the briny juice, then tear open the skin and relish the fleshy stem.

New season, just crushed, green extra-virgin olive oil Rather than fretting about festive purchases, the dedicated Better Foodie anxiously awaits the first sniff and taste, and the incomparable freshness, of the oil from their favourite single estate producer.

FESTIVALS

MAINE LOBSTER FESTIVAL, MAINE, US The prospect of contributing to the consumption of twelve tons of large-clawed crustacea is irresistible bait to the Better Foodie, as are the related shellfish shenanigans: a parade, music and the inevitable lobster-eating competition. (www.mainelobster.festival.com)

LA FIESTA DE LOS RABANOS, RADISH NIGHT, OAXACA, MEXICO Each December 23rd locals carve radishes into weird and wonderful shapes before feasting on rich fiery foods. There are also food stalls, music, dancing and fireworks to accompany the vegetable madness.

ST NICHOLAS DAY, VENETIAN ISLAND OF MURANO Celebrated with waterborne processions and feasting on December 11th.

CHANG MAI FOOD FESTIVAL, THAILAND A carnival atmosphere with food stalls offering arcane regional specialities.

CHRISTMAS MARKETS Espcially Strasbourg for bredele (a regional gingerbread); Nurembürg for lebküche (gingerbread), bratwurst and glühwein; Dresden, dating back to the 15th century – the place to purchase striezel (a kind of stollen); and Brussels for steaming mussels, preserved fruits and chocolate.

What should you expect if you're invited for zakuski?
Small Russian dishes – probably served with iced vodka

What spices are essential to garam masala?
Meaning 'strongly spiced mixed spices', garam masala always includes cardamom seeds (preferably a mix of green and black), black cumin seeds, black pepper, cinnamon stick, nutmeg, mace and cloves, and it should be freshly ground in a spice or coffee grinder.

Is it better to eat flat fish, such as Dover Sole, when they are roeing or not roeing?
Far preferable when not, as the flesh changes when the fish begins to roe becoming thinner, softer and not so good to cook

What language does the word 'bistro' come from and what does it literally mean?
It is from Russian bystro, meaning 'quick' and used by Russians in Paris during the Napoleonic wars who demanded their food be served quickly 'bystro, bystro!'

What is the name of the traditional wooden implement used to stir porridge?
A spurtle – a stirring stick shaped like half an elongated cricket bail; and the porridge should always be stirred clockwise.

What kind of risotto is traditionally served with osso buco?

Risotto alla milanese, flavoured with saffron. It is usually served with veal shanks stewed in rich tomato sauce, topped with gremolata.

What makes soufflé suissesse decadently rich?

It is made with Gruyère cheese and double cream.

What is a classic velouté?

A creamy sauce made with a roux and pale stock.

Should good quality dried porcini be pale and interesting or darker in colour?

Pale coloured stems and light brown caps are desirable. Darker pieces may have been oven-dried, which dissipates their light, delicate aroma.

What is mateolote?

A freshwater fish stew – often including anguilles (baby eels) – usually finished with button onions.

Acknowledgements

FIRST PUBLISHED IN 2006 BY
Quadrille Publshing Limited
Alhambra House
27–31 Charing Cross Road
London WC2H 0LS

Text © 2006 Sudi Pigott
Illustrations © 2006 Paul Bommer
Design and layout © Quadrille
Publishing Limited

EDITORIAL DIRECTOR Jane O'Shea
CREATIVE DIRECTOR Helen Lewis
EDITOR Laura Herring
DESIGNER Amanda Grapes
ILLUSTRATOR Paul Bommer
PRODUCTION Funsho Asemota

Cataloguing in Publication Data: a
catalogue record for this book is available
from the British Library.

ISBN-13: 978 184400 333 4
ISBN-10: 1 84400 333 7

Printed in Singapore

To my Mum, who made food important and enjoyable for me from the earliest age. Unwittingly my parents were Better Foodies well before the term was coined, and still are. My Aunt Jill, whose alluring collection of cookery books I wallowed in on every visit as a Better Foodie-in-the-making child. My long-suffering, deeply Foodie husband, Francis, and my perfect Foodie-in-the-making sushi-loving, eleven-year-old son, Theo, whose quirky epicurean insights have proved invaluable. My gorgeous god-daughter Flossie, who thinks I spend most of my time 'eating posh, proper chocolate, watching movies and going to restaurants' (if only …).

To friends who encouraged me to write the book, especially Jenni Muir, Lorna Wing, Frances Hopewell-Smith, Mario Wyn Jones, Benjamin Wooley, Judith Gifford, Lucinda Buxton, Phillip Owens, Venetia Jones (actually my lovely mother-in-law), Geraldine Laporta – all of whom are exemplary Better Foodies. To the many chefs, too numerous to mention, whose food has inspired me and furthered my epicurean curiosity, but particularly John Campbell of The Vineyard, John Williams of The Ritz, Peter Gordon of Providores, Heston Blumenthal of The Fat Duck, Simon Rogan of L'Enclume and Michel Roux of The Waterside Inn.

And not least to Clare Lattin of Quadrille for introducing me to Editorial Director Jane O'Shea, who immediately appreciated what the Better Foodie espoused, Laura Herring, my exemplary, calm and organised editor and Emily Sanders for sharing my boundless enthusiasm in publicising the book.